HANS

HANS

HOPE AMID NAZI SHADOWS

SHARI DRAKE

Outskirts Press, Inc.
Denver, Colorado

Outskirts Press, Inc.
http://www.outskirtspress.com

ISBN: 978-1-4327-5462-4

Outskirts Press and the "OP" logo are trademarks belonging to Outskirts Press, Inc.

PRINTED IN THE UNITED STATES OF AMERICA

Author's Note

I have heard brief accounts of my father's childhood all of my life. I have always struggled to frame the entire story because he had only offered it up in disjointed bits and pieces. Whenever a vivid memory surfaced, I watched him literally withdraw into another time and place. A haunted look would fill his eyes as he recounted a fragment of his past. I knew he had lost his father, my grandfather, in a war he did not agree with but was forced to take part in. When backed up against the cold hard wall of the Nazi regime, my grandfather had made a moral compromise to save the lives of his family. The best he could do to abide by his convictions was to insulate himself from the killing by becoming a medic. Overall, my father's formative years were not a time of carefree joy, but rather, an era of endurance.

In September of 2008, I traveled with my brother and parents to my father's homeland on a mission to encapsulate his past. We completed the final phase of the journey by train to the remote city of Krnov, Czechoslovakia, located within two kilometers of the current Polish Border. As the antiquated train rattled closer to our destination, the anticipation mounted. It was difficult to read my father's mood as it vacillated between cheerful expectation and quiet introspection as he canvassed the passing landscape. Each brief stop at the dilapidated train stations along our route increased the level of wariness and the encroaching feeling of trepidation was palpable. It was as if we were caught in a downward spiral whirling within the vortex of a time machine intent on hurling us back seventy years.

Hans returned to Jägerndorf (now known as Krnov, Czechoslovakia) in 2008 to revisit his childhood memories. He is standing at the train platform which is intricately tied to his past.

We disembarked the train under an overcast sky and stepped right into his earliest memories of that train station. The lens through which I was privileged to peer provided a clearer image of what my father had endured through a childhood fraught with a myriad of lost innocence. It was a surreal feeling to walk the same streets he had walked and immerse myself in his dialogue and culture. During this personally guided tour, I was surprised to hear that the buildings and streets were virtually unchanged from the time he raced barefoot among them. As we walked along the cobblestone walkways, we could still see the occasional unpatched bullet holes that had once riddled the sides of brick buildings. It occurred to me that the weathered buildings managed to withstand the ravages of fierce external forces, scarred but intact, just as my father had. I stood shoulder to shoulder with my father peering into the windows of his childhood school and could hear the echoes of his past surge over us. We paused on a bridge to take in the river rushing past us on its downward journey from the mountains. Of all the snippets of his past shared during my life, most of my father's most vivid stories were tied with this river. I was overcome by the intensity of experiencing this intricate piece of his past first hand. At that moment, I realized that, just as this river relentlessly swept through this resilient city, so does the blood of my forefathers thrum through my veins.

My brother and I took the opportunity to stroll through the park while our parents retired to the hotel for a rest. They were understandably exhausted from both the physical and emotional journey we had embarked upon. As we quietly sat on a cement park bench, I observed that the local people were quite reserved and looked at us suspiciously as they passed. We tried to fade into the scenery and look unobtrusive. My brother quietly pointed out that their facial features and coloring were remarkably similar to ours. Thanks to his insight, I took the time to study their appearance and mannerisms. After a period of contemplation, I could not deny the evidence of my roots which undeniably exist within the people of this unyielding city of Krnov.

My father has always been obsessed with fishing and putting food on the table. He butchered and bartered for various goods and services. He and my mom planted and tended a large garden which provided us with vegetables throughout the year. We were never rich, but had enough. He has always walked an unconventional path and has never been known for his tact in speaking his mind. To this day, he stockpiles supplies and is a masterful bargain hunter. I can now understand that he had been deprived of food and freedom so long that he never wanted to risk finding himself or his family reliving this fate. Food is more than nourishment to him; it is a symbol of triumph and a tangible form of hope. Freedom is not taken for granted by him; it is a cherished commodity bought at the high price of not only lost lives but trampled dreams.

Just like the loaves of rye bread he dearly loves, when

my father's outer crust is cracked, his softer, vulnerable side can be appreciated. My heart aches for the little boy who endured so much as a victim of so many circumstances outside of his control. I gaze at the pictures of the grandfather I never knew and feel an overwhelming sense of kinship. I am proud to be the daughter and grand daughter of these courageous men. It is to my father, and his father, that I dedicate this book. May I be worthy to print the fragile memories entrusted to my care, so that their sacrifice does not go undocumented. This story was written with my deepest love and respect as was told to me by my father, Hans.

Table of Contents

1

Casting Light Into The Shadows

My parents named me Hans Gustav as they welcomed me into the world over 75 years ago. I have lived with the memories of my childhood weighing heavy on my heart; a silent shadow trailing me through the years. The hope that sustained me through that era of my life has become entwined with the substance of who I have become. My eyes bore witness to horrors and intentional evil that invade my dreams still today. While it seems as though it happened in another life, to someone else, I can still connect the sounds, the smells, the tastes, with the movie reels replaying in the dark corners of my mind. While I still am able, I want to record my story, where my life began simply, innocently, yet was doomed to conform to a force I did not understand and was helpless to alter.

I've always wondered why no one told this story, for I did not live it in solitude. The Jews have always talked about the holocaust and how badly they were treated. I am not disputing this fact, but there is another side to it. Before the war erupted, many things were kept secret from the general German public. The Jews were known as the rich, the elite. They were hanging together back then and still do. The fact that they have historically stuck together as a cohesive group has allowed them to voice the loudest objections about the injustices Jews have endured. In contrast, the survivors of the rag tag group of which I belonged were scattered to the wind and basically lost touch with one another. Perhaps the silence was a result of the years submission forced upon us and the lingering fear of retribution. I've always doubted who would believe me, a lone voice speaking from a sliver of survivors, located in one city within the wide geographical expanse of World War II.

It wasn't just the Jews who were targeted; it was actually anyone who spoke against the Reich. We could not speak up against Hitler, and we took this to heart. We were young kids and knew that if we screwed up the whole family would be gone. All of these years I have kept these thoughts and memories bottled up because the fear of speaking was deeply ingrained within me as a child. I have never questioned the need to keep my mouth shut. As my years on this earth grow shorter, I am compelled to share another piece of the story from the silent victims of WWII and the Hitler war machine. Uncorking this bottle, these dark recollections bubble up to spark emotional pain and linger to taint my sleep with vivid nightmares.

2

A Storm Brewing

As a preschooler, I was too young to realize the massive political power play evolving in Europe. I had no idea that a tempest was brewing around me and that I would soon become steeped in it. I spoke at great lengths to my Aunt Josepha, my father's sister, who filled in the gaps for me much later in my life. I had only known her briefly as a boy because she had married and moved to Austria before the war at the urging of her family. As an adult, I did maintain contact with her until her death in 2008. I have gathered the following backdrop to my life based upon these conversations, research and my return trips to the land of my birth:

Adolf Hitler was born in Braunau am Inn, Austria, on April 20, 1889 - which was forty-five years before my birth. Amazingly, from this one man hatched an evil, strategic movement to empower Germany and systematically purify the German race. Although other countries may have left the door open by not resisting Hitler's Germany sooner or more fervently, in the end, it was Nazi Germany's actions that made WWII inevitable.

In November of 1921, Hitler was recognized as Fuhrer of a movement which was at that time only 3,000 members strong (Spielvogael, 2006). As I experienced first-hand, Hitler wanted to set himself apart from the political pack by focusing upon a distinctive calling card. He successfully developed his own branding via a unique Nazi symbol-the swastika- and the mandated Nazi greeting, "Heil!" Hitler then effectively boosted his personal power by establishing specialized squads whose sole mission was to maintain order at his meetings and to mitigate efforts made by all opponents. These elite squads matured into two distinct groups: the storm troopers (SA) organized by Captain Ernst Röhm and the Schutzstaffe (SS), Hitler's personal bodyguards whom were identified by the black shirts they wore (Spielvogael, 2006). The SA members that I personally encountered were the homegrown squad in charge of local control. The SA was mainly comprised of the older men like the bürgermeister (mayor) and city council members whose focus was on maintaining regional security. SS were the elite squad - young, with muscular builds and regimented minds that were unmoved by sympathetic pleas as they efficiently ensured compliance to the Reich. The SS were much more feared and when they arrived we knew someone was in for a major butt kicking.

A STORM BREWING

Entire families were wiped out at the brutal hands of the SS who never failed to leave death and ripples of terror in their wake. The grip of fear applied by these specialized forces served to maintain obedience among the citizenship and negated any stirrings of dissent.

It was disheartening to learn that, if not for the ruling of a sympathetic judge, Hitler would have been sentenced to death for treason. He was brought to trial after his failed attempt to seize power in November of 1923, during an armed uprising in Berlin known as *The Beer Hall Putsch* (Spielvogael, 2006). My entire life, as well as those of a multitude of others would have played out very differently if this course of events had been altered. As it turned out, his resulting five-year prison reprieve allowed him time to refine his strategy and write his autobiography, *Mein Kampf.* Upon his release, Hitler proceeded to carry out the master plan he had devised while incarcerated. He quickly rebuilt the scattered Nazi party and organized a whirlwind political campaign to gain prestige and power through acceptable routes rather than by force. His gift as a convincing speaker propelled him through the political process and he quickly became a household name. The ongoing economic depression further served to gain him acceptance of him among the dispirited unemployed who desperately wanted to believe in Hitler's idealistic dreams of creating a better Germany (Spielvogael, 2006). Bottom line- Hitler effectively presented himself as a symbolic lifeboat to a distressed nation sinking into a sea of despair under the weight of an economic policy teetering upon cataclysmic failure.

After a nationally run democratic vote, Adolf Hitler was appointed the Chancellor of Germany on January 31, 1933 (Jablonski, 1977). His secret goal was to eliminate democracy from Germany after using this exact same system to gain a seat of power. Hitler's plan would be accomplished by the creation of a "new authoritarian leadership to promote domestic unity" (Spielvogael, 2006). The crux of his plan placed a strong emphasis upon the indoctrination of the youth. According to his calculated blueprint for success, it was imperative that the will of the youth be properly bent to meet and sustain his objectives of world dominance. He was an adept orator whose lies were spoon fed to an audience starved for a message of hope. Between 1933 and 1939, Europeans idly watched as Adolf Hitler rebuilt Germany into a great military power (Jablonski, 1977). Sudetenland was offered up as a sacrificial lamb from Britain and France- with no input from either Russia or Czechoslovakia- in order to appease Hitler during his riveting diplomatic negotiations aimed at acquiring territory. Hitler's uncanny ability to feign sincerity served to assure the contingency that he had no further aspirations to expand his empire after gaining Sudetenland. Chamberlain actually went back to Britain and proudly announced that there would be "peace in our time" (Spielvogael, 2006). The future would eventually reveal Hitler's true intentions and the duped countries of Great Britain and France would live to regret their acquiescence.

Left to float alone, the Sudetenland people had no recourse but to abide by the new rules of Hitler or perish. Propaganda photos were distributed to relay the message of relief by the Suden-Deutch peoples, but these were all staged. Hitler did not tolerate dissent. Any resistance was met with complete annihilation by Hitler's military machine. As far as Hitler was concerned, military supremacy was essential for the creation of his distinct German empire poised to dominate not only Europe, but the entire world. All able-bodied men were drafted to serve in Hitler's military and adolescent males were required to attend Hitler youth meetings. Anyone even remotely resistant to these directives was visited by the SS and eliminated. The noose of Socialism that was cast over the necks of the Sudetenland peoples was jerked tightly and the country was literally in a death struggle.

If Hitler had succeeded in accomplishing his goals, I am positive the slimy tentacles of the Nazi New World Order would have elicited widespread brutal oppression for generations to come. The Nazis eventually lost, but not without immense sacrifice. I am forever thankful for the saving grace of the American and British soldiers who released us from the Nazi bonds. When the smoke cleared at the culmination of World War II, Europe essentially lay in ruin and a multitude of lives were changed forever.

HANS

Country borders were redrawn as governments regrouped. Like a massive deck of cards, the wounded people groups were reshuffled and left to deal with their scars and find some semblance of normalcy to resume their lives.

3

Humble Beginnings

Jägerndorf was a large industrial city in Sudetenland that was a strategic foothold because of its size and location right on the border of East Prussia, which is now Poland. It was a goal for Hitler to possess this area as part of his greater plans to expand Germany's *Lebensgtraum*, or living dream. The city of Jägerndorf actually had a long history of ownership squabbles between the Slavs, Russians, Poles and Czechs. This area was even part of Austria at one time, and then the Czechs came in, followed by the Germans. The city was a virtual gem tempting greedy neighboring countries to seize control for their own gain. Goods and workers flowed through the city known for its numerous textile factories, fertile farm lands, live stock farms and furniture factories boasting talented woodworking artisans like my father.

HANS

This is a photo of Jägerndorf, Sudetenland. It was most likely taken prior to the onset of the war. This photo was among the mementos saved by Ma.

I was born here -in Jägerndorf, Sudetenland, now known as Krnov in the Czechoslovakia Republic- on March 27, 1934. My nationality was Sudetendeusch. This area was a mixture of many different nationalities of peoples. Based upon the multiple dialects, I suppose it would be difficult for an outsider to tell exactly where I was living, but I always spoke German. The Czech and Bohemian people lived peacefully among us in this region. They worked side by side in amiable coexistence. From my point of view, there was never a distinction or visible prejudice between these multiple people groups before it was stirred up by Hitler. We were content, productive and did not seek the "assistance" of Germany-it was thrust upon us.

I was the middle child of three brothers, one was three years older and the other was three years younger than me. Out of respect for their desire of anonymity, I will not refer to them by name. My mother was a weaver in a factory, and my father was a carpenter that built wood furniture. He was quite skilled and began to work at the local organ factory where masterpiece organs were created to grace churches throughout the world. My parents both worked hard to provide a modest home for us within a small apartment. I know that we were never rich money wise but everything we had was earned through hard work and, therefore, pride.

My father was lean and tall, with an athletic build and a natural agility which suited him well as captain of his football team- referred to as soccer in America. His clear blue eyes reflected both intelligence and a self-less drive that I could not comprehend at the time, but of which I was drawn to like iron shavings to a magnet. I yearned to spend time with him, but I was too young and just didn't have the capacity to sit still so I usually was left behind. I never saw much of him because he typically left for work before I woke and returned after I was tucked into bed at night. His work schedule, coupled with the demands of his football team activities, left little time for him to spend with his family.

HANS

This is my parents' wedding photo, which was not dated. I estimate that they were married in 1929 or 1930. They look so young and innocent-with no idea what the future would hold.

My ma had it tough. She married my father roughly during the year of 1929 or 1930 (I never knew the exact date). Their first son was born in 1931. I think they were striving to get a home for the family, so were quite thrifty with their earnings. My mother spent more time with us than our father and was the disciplinarian. She was quick to use the strap to keep her rambunctious sons in line and safeguard their future by enforcing obedience. My older brother was sickly and my mother was easier on him because of his fragile nature. My younger brother was the baby of the family. Overall, I felt the sting of the strap more often because Ma expected more out of me. In today's world, I may have been labeled as having attention deficit disorder and perhaps medicated. Looking back, I realize that this persistent restlessness and my natural curiosity to figure things out, despite the consequences, was an important element to my overcoming barriers thrown before me throughout my childhood years. Honestly, I would describe myself as having been a little shit...but I am convinced now that this trait was the key to my being a survivor.

This is the only baby photo Ma had of me that survived the war. I named it "Goldie locks" because she loved my blond curls and did not want to cut my hair. The year 1934 is written on the back.

4

Failed Escape

As a four-year-old peering across the street at the Bahnhof (rail station) from my third floor apartment window, I was fascinated by the intriguing maze presented by the train tracks criss-crossing their way into the station. The trains rumbling into the station arrived and departed with clock-like precision which provided me with an unlimited source of entertainment and a unique perspective of my young world. I imagined where all of those people came from as I studied them emerging from the passenger cars and making their way across the platform. I ached to know where the passengers climbing up the steps to board the trains were headed. Daring destinations bubbled into my mind's eye as I wistfully watched the loaded cars disappear into the horizon leaving puffs of smoke in their wake. One day I hoped to be the one climbing aboard for a marvelous adventure.

The first sign of trouble was in early 1939, I remember there being lots of commotion. I was nearly five years old at that time. I observed that more people were leaving on trains than arriving. Many more Czech soldiers were noticeable in their bluish gray uniforms. The Czech soldiers had a flattened helmet topped with what looked like a rooster comb. In comparison, the German soldier's helmet looked more rounded helmet with ear muffs. The increased number of uniformed Czech soldiers raised my curiosity. I knew something was up.

There was an obvious sense of urgency in the crowds gathering on the train platform eagerly watching for the approaching train. Little time was wasted as the passengers hurried aboard and anxiously looked out the window as if they were fleeing some invisible demons. The demons were all too real, however, as I was soon to discover first hand.

When my father was home and speaking with Ma, I strained to hear the conversations through the thick walls. I usually could find out some good information if I was quiet enough. Something was amiss these past weeks, I was sure of it. I distinctly remember my father speaking of the Germans expected arrival and his hatred of Hitler. Sudetenland was literally handed over to Hitler in what was intended to be his final demand for land in September of 1938. He was glad that his sister was safely away in Austria as he earnestly spoke of escape plans for our family.

I remember walking to the back of the apartment

building where I saw my parents burning papers underneath the copper wash kettle where my ma usually did the laundry. My parents spotted me and told me to get back inside. When I ignored their request and asked what was going on, I was told that Hitler was coming. This was said with whispers and fearful visual scans of the area. Because I was just a young boy, no one bothered to offer me much information so I intently watched and listened. I remember seeing a lot of papers being burned beneath that kettle. When I asked why they were burning the papers, they finally gave in to my relentless curiosity. In hushed tones, I was told that my father was involved in a group. The papers must be burned, my ma explained, or there would be trouble when the Germans came. I thought it best to stop asking questions because I sensed the tension. My ma was holding back tears as she fanned the flames to consume the damning evidence.

I got the distinct impression that my father's life, as well as our own, was in jeopardy. Terror laced the whispers passing between them and worried glances gazed upward toward the acrid smoke wafting heavenward like a silent, redemptive prayer. A clear message was conveyed to me on that day - my father did not want anything to do with Hitler but the window of opportunity to impede him had been closed. Unbeknownst to me at the time, my father was a member of a resistance group whose mission it was to stop the advancement of the Nazis into the region. The football team he captained was a front for this underground organization. When the invasion appeared inevitable, all traces of the grass-roots rebellion were destroyed to safeguard the resistance members and their families. Only scorched remnants remained beneath the copper kettle when I somberly headed back into the apartment building, dragging my bare feet every step of the way. As I glance backward at that copper kettle scene in my mind, I see it as an ominous paradox depicting the black ashes of the failed Nazi resistance smoldering beneath sullied wash water that could not clean the looming grime away.

Since no one else in the family would watch over my grandfather when he became sick, he had been moved into our apartment so Ma could care for him. He was too ill to travel when the initial escape attempt was planned, so my parents postponed the trip. A week passed until he was fit to travel. Plans were put into motion when my father had received word that we had a chance to go to Canada. There was an urgency to move quickly. It didn't take long to pack up a bag of belongings and make our way down the three flights of stairs to the front of our building.

My ma told me that my father would be meeting us later and hurried us across the street to the bahnhof. We passed through the bustling station to stand on the platform with a crowd of others with similar plans. I remember peering eagerly down the train tracks with my brothers, mother and grandfather standing nearby. The air was thick with anticipation. I was excited that I actually had a

FAILED ESCAPE

ticket to board the train and could not wait to catch my first glimpse of the locomotive. A thrill ran up my spine as I spotted the dot on the horizon grow into the shape of a full engine billowing smoke as it rolled closer to where I stood.

The train proudly lumbered into the station and squealed to a stop. The few travelers crowding the exit to disembark were allowed to exit the train prior to my mother urging us to climb aboard. My father was in hiding, I don't know why, but he didn't get on the train with us. I knew better than to ask questions based upon the tense look on Ma's face. We found seats together and waited while others got settled. Finally, a whistle announced the start of the journey as the train slowly eased out of the station. I scoped out the car but did not see my father aboard. The porter made his way through the cars checking and stamping tickets. I divided my attention between what was going on inside the car and watching the landscape pass by outside as the train chugged down the rails. The rolling farmland was bordered by small rock walls to denote ownership, but it was too early in the year for the crops to be peeking from the dirt. My breath left fog on the cold window as I silently rocked with the rhythm of the train and counted the tunnels we passed through. At this point, the destination was not a concern for me, I was enjoying the journey. The only nagging thought bouncing around my young mind was the uncertainty of my father's whereabouts.

HANS

I don't know how far we got down the tracks when the sound of gun shots shattered the tranquility that nearly lulled me to sleep. The train abruptly stopped with the angry screech of brakes grating against the rails. I was lurched forward as I held tight to the window casing to avoid becoming unseated. As we came to a stop, the train quickly became surrounded by German soldiers. Loud voices pierced the silence as the passengers collectively held their breath and clutched the hands of loved ones. Orders were shouted for us to get off the train if we knew what was good for us. Ma silently nodded at us to follow her and Grandfather as we left the train with our meager belongings. We were herded away from the train and directed to wait as the remainder of the passengers were cleared from the cars. Soldiers boarded the train and carefully swept through each car to ensure everyone had gotten off. The resounding clash of boots on the floorboards and the clang of doors being harshly slammed shut during the search heightened the sense of finality to the trip.

When the armed guards seemed satisfied that everyone was off the train, we were escorted toward a nearby factory. I occasionally glanced around the group making their way over the rutted road, but still did not see my father. A sick feeling filled the pit of my stomach as I realized our escape to freedom was over and I had no idea where my father was. No one uttered a sound. The thud of muffled footsteps against the newly thawed ground accompanied us on our forced hike. I could hear my heartbeat setting a tempo in my ears as my heart felt like jumping out of my chest.

When we arrived at the seemingly abandoned factory the doors were flung open and we were bluntly ordered to get inside. Scattered sunlight speared through broken windows and bounced off the haze of dust stirred by shuffled steps. After shouting out instructions that we were to stay put, the guards broke apart to guard the exits and some lit up cigarettes as they enjoyed a break. They shared food rations amongst themselves but we were not given any food or water. We found a spot on the floor for our family unit. Ma helped Grandfather, still weak from his recent illness, sit down and motioned for us to join him. We knew without being told that we should keep our mouths shut and not draw any attention to ourselves.

We slept on the bare floor that night with just the few clothes we had on and no blanket. It was a weird feeling, because I had slept in my own bed just the night before and here I was sleeping on a hard, dirty floor that smelled rank. The warmth of my little two-year-old brother, snuggled trustingly next to me, strengthened my resolve to stay calm. I quietly watched the soldiers from the corner of my downcast eyes so I would not be caught unaware in case the guards tried something. Eventually, I fell into a fitful sleep as I relived the unsuccessful escape trip in my dreams.

I was nudged awake the next morning by the boot of one of the soldiers making their way through the mounds of sleeping captives. I sat up and caught the eye of Ma who urged me to get up and quickly gather my things. The factory doors were flung open by the guards and we began another hike. This time our destination was a local train station further down the same road we took the day before. My ma, straddled by Grandfather and my older brother led the way. I held my little brother's hand as we made our way through the mist of early dawn as the trill of bird song was in sharp contrast to our current circumstance. Armed escorts loosely encircled the group to ensure no stragglers were lost on the trip or that no one dared to break away.

The next thing I remember, we were loaded and headed back to Jägerndorf on a different train. This time, we were continually watched by the German military whose presence was notable in each car. This train ride lacked the sense of expectation of yesterday and I found no joy in watching the passing landscape. Upon our arrival into the familiar Jägerndorf station, I was surprised that we were allowed to leave with merely a stern warning not to try leaving again or else things would go badly for us. Not waiting for them to change their mind about letting us go, we quickly got off the train and hurried away.

We walked across the street to our apartment only to discover that someone else had moved into our old apartment during our short time away. We were bluntly told to get lost and had no recourse. We weren't even allowed to gather any of our modest furnishings left behind. We were now officially homeless, with only our meager belongings to call our own. We had nowhere to go, so we found a park bench and stayed put. For the time being, my restless five-year-old spirit was tamed by the shock of not knowing what the future held. My world had taken a tail spin and I had yet to recapture my balance. So, I put on a brave face for my little brother and patiently waited it out.

5

Starting Fresh

The same day we became homeless, my dad somehow found us and revealed his revised plan that would start a new chapter in my life. He carefully laid out his new strategy after a joyous reunion filled with hugs, reassuring smiles and a few tears from my ma. To this day I am not sure if he had been on that train with us or not, he never discussed it. I was surprised to learn that during the time we were separated he had discovered he lost his job at the organ factory. Very calmly, my father explained that the owner of the factory, who happened to be a Jew, had just disappeared. Without warning, the entire factory was shut down and the doors barred. A notice posted on the doors informed workers that the factory was closed. As quickly as that, my father was suddenly among hundreds of workers seeking a means of income.

If our escape had been successful, all these issues

would have been left far behind us, but, since we were now stuck in Jägerndorf, we had no recourse but to deal with the situation. This juncture became the tipping point at which time the Nazi regime seized control of my country, my town, and my life. The switch had been thrown and the cylinder of socialism had become firmly locked in place. The freedoms enjoyed under the formerly capitalistic society were shrugged off and replaced by the heavy yoke of socialism. The expectations were clear; it was the duty of all to work for the betterment of society which was to be determined solely by the German government. The German occupiers were heralded as the savior for our people. With Hitler at the helm, there was no dissention allowed. It was one voice, one cause and one collective mission. Individuality was squashed beneath the booted heel of the German war machine, hell bent on taking over the world.

Always one to think quickly on his feet, my father had scurried to find a solution before finding us at the train station. With the plans to flee the area vanquished, he knew he had to devise an alternative plan. After scouting out his options, he had gone to see the owner of a furniture factory where he secured both a job and a roof over our heads. He explained to us that he had made arrangements for the whole family to live in a factory housing complex located about six kilometers away from the train station, in the country. Father had made furniture at this same factory years prior, so the owner knew him and his work well. The fact that my father had a good reputation helped him get the job. The factory was no longer building furniture, however, because it was being converted into making ammunition boxes for Hitler. Knowing the deep-seated hatred my father held for Hitler, I knew that working to promote his cause was a huge moral concession. Even at my young age, I realized the sacrifice of principles he was making to work at this military support factory on behalf of the family.

Our reunited family trekked to our new home with little more than the clothes on our backs and a few belongings in the sacks we carried. But somehow, with my father leading the way with my baby brother hoisted on his shoulder, I felt a spring in my step that had been missing hours earlier. It seemed as though everything would be alright, somehow, as long as we were together even though there was a definitive sense that evil lurked in the shadows.

HANS

This is the only family photo I know to exist. It was taken in August of 1939 while we were living in factory housing outside of Jägerndorf. I would have been five years old. I am standing front and center, flanked by my two brothers. My father's stepmother and sister are standing between my parents in the back row.

A new pattern of normalcy settled upon my family, at least for a while. My dad worked at the factory every day. Ma continued working at the textile factory, but now making uniforms for the military instead of clothing. I went to school six days a week with my younger brother and the other children in the building. We became acquainted with one another on these long walks to and from school and began to solidify a kinship with one another. My older brother always went his own way with the older kids, so he was not a part of this group.

We slowly got accustomed to our new surroundings

in our makeshift home in the factory housing unit which was laid out like a large apartment building. It was a two story building with ten apartments on each floor. Each of the apartments had two rooms, a bedroom and a kitchen area that was the multi-purpose area. A wash room was located on each floor which all families could use as a utility room. Our biggest area was outside where each family had one woodshed to use as they pleased and a spot to plant a garden.

The apartment building was actually quite sophisticated compared to our previous one. This one had indoor toilets at the end of the hall to share with the other apartments on the same floor. The water filling the overhead tank for the toilet came from a cistern in the building's basement. The cistern was filled from rain water collected in gutters off of the roof and diverted to the basement. A small amount of water swished the bowl clear with a pull of the chain. I'm not sure where it went from there, but I think it went underground to a sewage ditch. In the winter months, we found it was too cold to make it down the hall, so we mostly just peed in a bucket. It was one of the many daily chores to take the full bucket outside to dump in a spot designated for this duty. The water for cooking came from a pump outside. We hauled this water indoors in another bucket of course. Any water from dishwashing we had to carry back out to dump. My younger brother and I hauled the water, it was one of our chores and we thought nothing of it.

HANS

The laundry was washed in a community kettle by boiling it, and this was a family chore. There wasn't any soap to clean the clothes; just the boiling water. We would then rinse the clothes in the stream which was downstream from the clothing factory. At times the factory would release dye into the stream and it would turn the water different colors so our clothes would get some color too. This made it sort of fun to see everyone wearing clothes with various tints of color. The washed clothes would then be spread out in the grassy area to be bleached in the sun. We would sprinkle extra water from a watering can on any stains and the sun would bleach them out. There was also a wash line, but this had to be coordinated with many families so we usually just laid them on the grass. It was a gamble to use the clothes lines anyway because clothes would frequently be "lost" and it became the cause of many arguments.

In the winter, we had to protect the water pump from freezing. We put straw around it and tied it on with rope. It looked like a straw dummy when we were done with it. If the pump would freeze, no one would have water so it was important to insulate it from the cold. On several occasions it still managed to freeze, in that case we had to walk down the road to a neighboring well to get water.

This new routine did not last for long. One day my mother was crying and I got that sick feeling in the pit of my stomach again. Through her sobs, we were told my father was drafted into the German Air Force. We were allowed to stay in the factory housing, but he would have to report, he had no choice. He hated Hitler to the core of his being, of this I am positive. He made another great sacrifice for us, the ultimate gesture of a loving father forced to choose between his core beliefs and his family's well-being. He didn't want to fight, but was told that the whole family would be shot to death if he didn't. The ominous existence of the black-shirted SS was a prominent reminder that there was no doubt to the sincerity of this threat.

He was drafted in the year 1939. He opted to go into the German medical core so he wouldn't have to carry a gun. This small concession also allowed him the peace of mind knowing he would be helping save lives, not end them. In order to be in this core, he was sent to France for training. After the completion of training, he was told he'd be stationed in Greece. My father was an even-tempered, peace-loving man. The only time I ever was scolded by him was when I burned a hole in the wood floor to make a spot to play marbles. I deserved the scolding.

When the day arrived for him to leave, he said his goodbyes with a long embrace for each one of us and a reminder to behave for Ma. He tried to reassure me with a smile that all would be well in the end, but I could not help but feel as though my life was crumbling before my eyes. We watched him leave as my mother cried uncontrollable sobs of despair. She was left alone with the three of us; she had to work full time to pay the rent and provide

HANS

for us. I'm not sure how much the German Reich paid the families left behind, except that it wasn't enough. This started another chapter in my life. My father was gone and my mother began working longer hours in a factory sewing uniforms for the German military. This left us pretty much alone to fend for ourselves.

This is a photo of my father, Gustav, after he was drafted into the German Air force in 1939. He is the one sitting, looking as though the weight of the world is on his shoulders along with the hand of an unknown soldier.

6

Schooling Under The Swastika

In 1940, at six years of age, I was in first grade. I had a fraulein teacher who was very strict because she wanted to make good Germans out of us. It was her job to conform us to the standards of the Reich and she took this mandate very seriously. Her boyfriend was a tank officer. She was proud of him and spoke of him frequently, going so far as to read parts of his letters to the class. He was portrayed as a model for us to strive for, a shining example of how it was the highest honor to be in Hitler's service. His picture was posted right below Uncle Adolf's at the front of the classroom. Every day we had to stand next to our desks and respectfully salute the pictures. This ritual was followed up by singing. The fraulein insisted we sing the song proclaiming the superiority of Germany. So, every day we had to stand next to our desks and hold our right arm up through the entire singing of, "Deutschland über alles" (Germany over all).

HANS

Each student had a slate board that was about 10 x 12 inches with a wooden frame. We carried this to and from school in a hard backpack. The slate had a wooden frame to protect it from breakage if dropped. One side had solid lines for writing and the other was blank for arithmetic. There was a hole in the frame for a rag which was used to wipe the slate clean. I didn't use paper until third grade.

One painful lesson for me was writing. I was born left-handed and the teacher fiercely stated that left-handers were not allowed in Germany. I was relentlessly lectured that Germans were the superior race and they had to be perfect. I was told that I had to change. Since I tried but could not write well with my right hand, I would be harshly disciplined for my lousy hand writing. In an effort of self-preservation, I would try to sneak writing with my left hand then switch back when she was watching. She was sharp and I was not always fast enough to switch hands, so I would get smacked with a board and humiliated before the class when she caught me. This was a very frustrating time for me because even at my young age I could not understand why I was beaten for something that just came natural to me. Because of this stringent "training" in my formative years, I am ambidextrous to this day.

I went to school six days a week in a "cloister" monastery school from the first through fourth grades. School was Monday through Friday from eight to five and on

Saturday for a half a day. I tried to sneak out of religion classes when I could by making up excuses or just sliding out a window to make my escape. The religion classes were just extensions of the daily schooling of indoctrination. Basically, it was drilled into us that God wanted us to be obedient to the Third Reich. We had school until 10:00 am on Saturday mornings, so Saturday and Sunday were play days. We were supposed to go to church on Sunday, but Ma never went with us so we'd play soccer instead. We had to be careful to wash off any mud or grass stains before going home, of course, so Ma wouldn't get angry with us. But Ma was usually too exhausted from her long work days to have the energy to check up on us and we took full advantage of this one full day of freedom.

One of the most prominent memories I have from my time in the cloister schule was the day I saw Hitler with my own eyes. We were told the day ahead to come dressed in a white, short sleeved shirt and short black pants. I really am not sure if I was wearing shoes that day or not because I went to school without shoes all summer long. The greatest thing about that day is that we got to skip the cod liver oil treatment because he was expected to come before the scheduled time we had to take it. I hated taking that cod liver oil and we had to take a spoon full every day. It was part of the regimented routine; we lined up and took turns opening our mouths in front of the teacher who gave us each a heaping spoonful of that vile stuff. We all used the same spoon so cleanliness was not a consideration. Looking back, this practice probably helped me stay healthy despite my poor diet. Anyway, this day we got a free pass on the cod liver oil.

We were marched in a single file from the school to the town square where we were lined up to face the staging area. The girls were given flowers and positioned in the front of the boys to greet Hitler. I later learned Hitler loved the little girls and used pictures of them giving him flowers as part of his propaganda scheme while, at the same time, stroking his ego. The girls were given instructions on how to approach our guest of honor including the proper way to bestow the flowers upon him with a curtsey and a smile. The boys were drilled on the importance of staying in their assigned spot and to greet the supreme leader with a salute while keeping their eyes straight ahead, all the while standing at attention. The older residents of the city were congregated behind the children. I couldn't help but think we were merely puppets in a great performance.

With nothing but time to waste and an active mind to occupy, I scanned the scene from my vantage point. The scrubbed cobblestone streets were lined with German and SS flags flapping in the wind and flowers spilled from the window boxes adorning the parade route. The flag pole holders had been hastily installed in evenly spaced intervals, about 20 meters apart, on each building within a couple of days prior to Hitler's arrival. Of this I am certain because I knew Jägerndorf like the back of my hand and I knew these flag brackets were not there before. I was amazed how quickly these flags and the stage were installed despite the financial hardships endured by the city's inhabitants. This fact seemed to hammer home how important a man Hitler was because everyone was scrambling to pay homage to him or was afraid to do otherwise.

I had to wait for what seemed like forever standing shoulder to shoulder with the other boys in my class under the blistering mid-day sun. The motorcade was at least an hour and a half late but we were forbidden to leave or even sit down. The teacher kept a sharp eye on us and we dared not break rank. I had to pee and held it as long as I could with a painful effort. Finally, I just spread my legs and let loose onto the cobblestones. There was definitely an advantage to not wearing any underwear and having loose pants on. I don't know what the girls did but I remember seeing quite a few puddles left by other boys so I knew that I was not alone in my decision to just give up and let go.

The ominous motorcade of black Mercedes limousines finally arrived with great fanfare and rolled to a stop in front of the staging area. With military precision the SS approached the motorcade and stood at attention. After several minutes, the rear door of the second vehicle was opened wide. I then realized Hitler wasn't in the first car which everyone was focused on. There was a decoy car out in front just in case someone plotted against the Führer. Hitler emerged from the blackness of the car and regally walked past the SS honor guard, with an answering salute, toward the stage.

My first impression was that Hitler looked like a shrimp. He tried to walk tall to make up for his short stature, I thought, but it didn't work. He made his way past the assembly with a measured gait and a stern, purposeful look affixed upon his face. One of his cronies placed a step behind the podium for him to stand on so he would look taller than the rest of his entourage on the stage. I was not fooled because I could tell he was shorter than all of them while he was walking up there. They must have thought we were stupid not to notice.

Six of his closest advisors were all standing next to him with grim faces and stiff backs as their eyes scanned the crowd. I did not know the names of all of his backup gang, but I did recognize Herman Göhring, in an olive green airforce uniform, from pictures we were shown in school. Göhring looked like a big fat barrel to me with his round chest and big belly that could not be disguised under his uniform. Another advisor was dressed in a SS uniform covered in medals. The newspaper later posted a picture of the event in which another advisor was identified as Himler. Wearing a dark suit and rimmed glasses, he looked out of place without a uniform on. I had no clue what these men represented except that they emanated a shivering gust of arrogance and evil.

SCHOOLING UNDER THE SWASTIKA

The speech delivered by Hitler was memorable because of how offensive it seemed to me. He shouted into the microphone that was inches from his mouth. His voice was unbelievably loud as the crass message assaulted my ears. The stage was setup by the Rathaus (city hall) which was located in the town square below the courthouse bell tower. Hitler's harsh voice echoed as it bounced off of the brick buildings surrounding the square. I ached to cover my ears to muffle the onslaught of the words which were pummeling my eardrums like bullets from a Tommy gun. I dared not move so I was at the mercy of the orator with the screeching voice. The heart of the message was that the time had come for Germany to be the supreme leader of the world and victory was within our grasp. The youth, Hitler insisted, were given the distinct honor to carry out the assigned mission to ensure Germany would remain the world's dominant force.

After this shouting match ended and the echoes died away to stark silence, Hitler stood for a moment to appraise the crowd and paused to seemingly let the message sink in. There was no opportunity to ask questions and absolutely not even a whimper of protest heard from the crowd. Then, amid a chorus of "Heil Hitler" from the saluting throng, Hitler abruptly stepped off of his perch and departed from the stage. During the booted march back to his big black Mercedes, the girls curtsied respectfully before Uncle Adolf and handed him bunches of fresh wildflowers. He paused to pat a young girl upon her braided head as he accepted her flowers. He probably felt tall next to the small girl which gave his mustached smile a smidgen of sincerity. With a final sharp wave to the crowd he disappeared into the car and, with the muffled thud of the closing door, the motorcade promptly left our city. We were not allowed to move until the shiny glare of sunshine reflecting off the polished chrome bumpers of the motorcade disappeared into the distance. It was with a mixed sense of relief and bewilderment that I mutely returned to school with my classmates. I could not help but wonder what the future held and I sent a silent prayer for my father's protection-wherever he was. Without a doubt, I knew my father was an unwilling participant in this haughty military machine of destruction that appeared to be gaining strength. I held fast to the nugget of hope that, given time, good would overcome evil.

7

Rotten Relatives

We had blood relations living in the same town but that was not to our advantage. My mother was hopeful that she could receive some help from them but we were never welcomed there. If we went to visit one of them, and they knew about it ahead of time, they would lock the doors so they didn't have to let us in. I remember looking at an upstairs window while my ma was knocking at the door and seeing a drape pulled aside. I knew they were inside peeking at us, but refused to even open the door to find out why we were there.

They all refused to help with my sick grandfather who ended up living with us until his death in 1941. My grandfather, who was a Bohemian, was a tinsmith all of his life. His wife died in 1939. After that time he needed help and could not live alone. The poor guy took a shot of Slivovitz, a plum brandy, every morning for breakfast to keep him going. I am not sure what exactly was wrong with him, but I remember standing at the graveside at his funeral. All of Ma's sisters showed up for the ceremony and then came to our apartment to fight over his meager belongings afterward. It was quite a sight watching them tearing each other's hair out over some lead vases and polished Czech crystal. This was the one and only time they graced our humble home with their presence.

This is one of my all-time favorite photos. Ma's father and step-mother are proudly posing in front of their garden shed in bare feet. I am unsure of the year it was taken, but it was sometime prior to her death in 1939.

The sad part was that my mother's sisters and their husbands were all better off than us but they were selfish. The husbands had various disabilities so they didn't have to go to war. One had tuberculosis, one had his leg amputated after it was pinched between rail cars and the other was sickly looking because he was a heavy smoker. My mother had five sisters living, one had died. The other three lived nearby and were named Mitzi, Hilde and Hedwig. The other two lived farther away -Tante Olga, in Millington, Michigan, and Tante Anna who had a little store in Vienna, Austria. At the time, no one wanted to help us out, or accept us, or even give us a good meal. The only exception was Tante Mitzi, my mother's second oldest sister, who gave us some baked goods on the rare occasion she could get it to us on the sly. Her domineering husband would not allow it if he had known. Basically, even amongst our family, we were outcasts. So, in the end, we just had to take care of ourselves and use our own abilities to survive.

8

Self-reliance

At the time, the German government issued stamps for a food allotment once a month. Different colored sheets were distributed to the head of each family and were only valid for the month indicated. Green or yellow stamps were for adults and blue stamps were for children. We had to watch how many stamps we used so we would have enough to eat for the entire month. Since we were a family of four, we tried to get by on one sheet of stamps per week. Ma would cut the stamps out with scissors and entrusted the stamps to me to carry to the market since she worked all of the time. I knew I would get a beating if I messed up, so I was very careful with the stamps. Use of these stamps allowed for the following exchange of perishable goods: 4 quarts of whole milk for each child, ¼ pound of butter or cheese, ¼ pound of sugar, and so many grams of flour or baked bread which amounted to 5 - 6 pounds for our family in a month. If we were lucky we could sometimes get cottage cheese instead of milk. In addition, the stamps allowed a monthly total of 2 pounds of meat or sausage. If we got lucky, we could get twice the amount of horse meat instead of beef if it was available. This would occur if a farmer had a lame or old horse slaughtered. For a special treat we would get a ring of horse bologna. One-fifth of the meat we received was bones which we used to make soup.

This is a scan of my father's actual fishing license. It was issued to him while on military leave in February of 1942. This license allowed him to fish in a designated 2 kilometer section of the river. The fact that the Germans insisted upon fishing licenses during wartime demonstrates their passion for detailed documentation and the absolute control exerted over every facet of our lives.

Money wasn't plentiful so we subsidized by growing and scrounging for food. The main food was a variety of soup and rye bread. Ma always insisted we get the two-day old bread so it would last longer and we wouldn't get as hungry if we ate it. For breakfast we made garlic toast on a hot plate by rubbing garlic and salt on the toast. If my mother worked on the farm in the summer, she would get some tallow and we scraped a little of that on it. I have to admit that once in a while my cravings would get the better of me and I got a mouth-watering loaf of fresh bread instead. I just had to weigh out my options and decide at the time if it was worth the beating I would ultimately receive.

We had a little garden to grow extra vegetables and supplement our food stores. Each family had a garden plot staked out in the courtyard area of our apartment building that was approximately fifteen by ten feet in size. We never stole from the gardens of other families in the complex because they were watched very closely plus, we knew we were all in the same boat. We planted a row of carrots, kohlrabi, cabbage, parsley, dill, peas, radishes, spinach and a full row of poppies. Garlic was planted in the fall and allowed to stay underground over winter. In the spring it would grow and we would have big plants of it. The garlic could grow next to other garden goods without interfering.

Spinach was a main source of nourishment for us. We would go to the river to pick young nettles, a green leafy plant, to make the spinach from our garden go farther. A mix of 20% spinach to 80% nettles was cooked together with a few potatoes. We would add a little flour, if lucky, to thicken it a little and make it more filling. If we were fortunate enough to have eggs from our own chickens, one would be split between the four of us. We ate lots of soup, it went the farthest and water could always be added to stretch it.

We didn't have room to grow potatoes in our small garden, so those we stole when the opportunity presented itself. My younger brother and I were allowed to help the local farmer pick potatoes instead of going to school. A machine slung out the rows, it was our job to put them in willow baskets after we picked them off the ground. The farm maids would pick up the baskets to take them away. As we walked, we would step on some nice potatoes and push them into the ground to cover them. Then we would return after a good rain to collect those potatoes. The white tops of the potatoes were easy to spot with the dirt washed away. We would get a couple bags that way for use through the summer. We received a family allotment of 50-75 lbs of potatoes in the fall for use during the winter. To keep the potatoes warm, we would put straw between the boards in our little hallway storage closet to try to keep the potatoes from freezing. We would end up eating frozen potatoes anyway despite our efforts, but it helped. They got sweeter when frozen, and tasted awful, but it was still food.

During the summer months this area had a short growing season so it was important to gather goods and store them for the winter. We had a cloth bag, like a pillow case, that held dried food stuff that we used for cooking over the long bitter winter months. There was one bag each of dried poppy seeds, mushrooms, garlic, and chicory which was used to make strong coffee. The poppies we grew were allowed to dry and then we popped the tops off. After the stalks were completely dried, we would break them and shake out the seeds. My mother would make dumplings and add the poppy seeds for flavor. If she had some flour, she would bake mokuchen which was a poppy seed pastry, but this was rare. We never had many baked goods because it was a luxury.

We stacked up food our own way. My little brother and I went into the fields after they were cut and raked searching for barley, oats or wheat stalks missed by the thresher. We would pick the grain heads off, one by one, and stick them in a pillow case. For days after harvest, we would scour the fields for this booty. We would rub off the grain by hand and then save the straw. We used the grains for our own food and for feed for our animals. We also ground some flour by pounding the various grains into a powder using smooth river rocks. By winter, we had saved up 20-25 pounds of grain through our efforts.

We used ground barley instead of coffee beans and always had a pot of brown brew on the stove. This brew was created by toasting barley kernels in the wood stove until they were dark brown and then grinding these kernels with a block of chicory. The chicory gave it a brown color and a taste similar to coffee when it simmered in water. The brown brew was always in a kettle on the stove, we just had to add more water as it thickened. Sometimes, we added a little milk to the coffee, but sugar was hard to come by. The milk we received from the monthly stamps amounted to a gallon a week, but we didn't have a refrigerator to keep it from spoiling. The basement steps leading toward the cistern were cool so that's where we kept the milk. We usually used it up in a couple of days because it soured quickly.

The straw remaining after we meticulously got all of the grain off of the stalks was used for our collection of livestock as well as for natural insulation. We usually kept six to nine chickens and one rooster. We ended up trading our rooster for another rooster to get a new blood line started and better layers. The straw was used to create nests for the laying hens. We let them loose in the yard to search out their own food but kept a close watch on them. We also fed the chickens from the grain bag if we needed to supplement their diet to fatten them up and keep them laying eggs. When a chicken didn't lay any more eggs, we had a feast. Each butchered chicken provided three to four meals for us. We ate everything, even the head. We also kept three breeding pairs of rabbits that bedded down in the straw. We butchered and roasted the young rabbits for a special treat or used them to barter for other items. Again, we used every bit of the rabbits, even the heads and feet for soup. We kept the breeding rabbits, two females and one male, alive through the winter so we would keep the supply of young rabbits coming. We also kept about six laying hens-as many as we had feed for-and the rooster alive until spring, We would put the hens to work sitting on 10-12 eggs in the spring so we could get a new brood of chicks started. In all of my life I never had enough meat; I always had to portion it. To this day I enjoy every bite of meat that I have the privilege of sinking my teeth into and eat all of the leftovers.

We also kept geese for both food and warmth. When the geese began to molt, we plucked the feathers to fill our feather bed and plump it up every year. We had to pluck the feathers away from the goose or risk tearing the skin. If this happened, we ate goose for a week. The electricity cost too much, so Ma only let us use one light bulb. We also stretched the wood and coal by keeping the apartment frigid, especially while we slept. The fluffy goose down covering served to keep us warm through the long winter months. When my father was home all three of us slept in one bed, otherwise, my younger brother slept with Ma while I slept with my older brother. We used each other's body heat to stay warm.

We force fed the geese to fatten them up and make sure they would have big livers. Ma would use the barley grain we had gathered out of the field for this purpose. She added water to the ground barley and rolled the dough into logs. These logs were then jammed down the geese's throat twice a day. She would massage the neck to make sure the barley dumplings made the trip from the gullet to the stomach. When we butchered the plumped up goose, the livers alone would be big enough to make us several nourishing meals. Of course we kept close tabs on our prized geese to make sure they didn't end up in someone else's pot. During one winter, we tried to keep one goose penned up under the stove. One day the goose got loose and we chased it all over the apartment. The goose ended up on top of the hot stove where it danced wildly as its feet were toasted. When ma got home from work, we really caught hell after she saw the aftermath of goose pursuit and its scorched feet.

Time went on. I did not track it by a calendar, but rather by the season. In the summer we picked berries, wild cherries, and hunted for mushrooms in the wooded area. We would also pick various leaves - blackberry leaves, St. John's Wort, (we called it Joneskraut), Basswood blossoms- we would bag it all up and dry these leaves to make tea.

When we walked to the woods, my brother and I passed a small flour mill on the East Prussia side of the river (now Poland). Most of the time the miller gave us some floor sweepings of flour that he kept in a barrel by the door. He charged 25 Fennig or about 6 cents for a measured portion of this treasure. We always carried a small paper bag for this purpose and were careful not to spill any on the walk home. Some times we gave the miller some mushrooms or berries we had collected, in that case we did not have to pay for this flour. This all helped to get food on the table and filled our bellies.

We visited our neighborhood market to gather some

other items. The woman working there was pretty slow and we used this to our advantage. We waited outside the store until other customers entered the store. When it was his turn, my brother would wait in line and ask for an item like yeast or sugar that they didn't have anyway to act like we were there for a reason. While the other customers or my little brother kept the lady behind the counter occupied, I would help myself to the goods. The salt or oatmeal was stored in large quantities on the shelf below the counter on the other side of the wall. I would pull the nail, like an oversized thumb tack, out of the board under the counter top while the lady was preoccupied. I would sneak some of whatever was available, put it under my loose coat, and put the board back the way it was. I used my hands while leaning against the counter, so no one suspected what I was really doing. After the lady informed my brother that she did not have the item he asked for, we strolled out of the store. I never took enough that it would be missed, similar to robbing a bank for $5.00. We were careful not to take much or visit too often to raise suspicion. This was our "honey hole."

The basics of what we wore all summer long, was a pair of shorts with a rubber band to hold them up, no shirt, no shoes and no underwear. We only had one pair of shoes for the winter with long stockings to keep our legs covered. It was very cold in that area when winter arrived. We stayed bare foot all summer long, from May to September. We would even go bare foot to school. We saved our shoes for cold weather to make them last unless there was a special occasion to bring out the shoes. We had one bicycle in the family. The bike had corks around the wheel rim instead of an inner tube. It was real simple to fix a flat. If a cork popped out from hitting a hole in the road, it was easy to just stop and push in a replacement from the stash in our pockets. We had to share the bicycle, so most of the time we walked.

Christmas in Jägerndorf...

Usually from the middle of November we tried to be good because we knew on December 6th we would be getting visitors. This was the date Saint Nickolas arrived during the dark of night with his sidekick Rumpelmann, also known as the devil. This duo represented the ultimate judgment of good and evil. My little brother and I were scared shitless. The white bearded Saint Nick usually knew all about us and we did not get any candy, apples or nuts. We had no argument about that, even though our older brother received these goodies. What worried us was escaping from the fate of Rumpelmann. The chain rattling Rumpelmann was dressed in black raggedy clothes, looking like a tramp, with his face painted blood red. This grim reaper had a sack slung over his shoulder which we were told was filled with the very bad children, who would shrink up upon being tossed into the sack. These shrunken children would be taken along by Rumpelmann and lost forever. We felt fortunate to just get swatted on the hind end with a willow reed and handed a lump of coal rather than being added to his sack. As this menacing visitor left, he warned us that we better shape up or he would be taking us along next year. We feared this devil man and were very happy we could stay around for another year. I guess Ma gave him the inside scoop and this allowed her another way of trying to keep us in line. After our fright night, we looked forward to Christmas.

Christmas was quite an exciting time for us. The highlight of the celebration was having a carp dinner. Our town had an ice skating ring for winter entertainment. At the end of the year, our town would catch all the Carp out of this lake before it froze and everyone could get so many pounds of Carp. Because we had four people to feed, we would get a 4-5 pound carp for our Christmas dinner. We would make sure we would get our carp when they first were available and then we would keep it alive in our bath tub. We then wouldn't have to take a bath for about three weeks which was a great treat for us. Most of the time the bath water was luke warm at best and there was not much soap available to clean with anyway, so it was no big loss.

Getting ready for Christmas was a special time for us. We would put a few bulbs and glitter out to make it look festive. We cut down a small tree, about three foot high, from the woods and would sneak it home. We had to hide it in a burlap sack, all tied up, so the forester or police wouldn't see us take it out. We would have to cover our trail in the snow by walking backwards out of the woods. We would decorate the tree with clothespins with a cup on top to hold a small candle. We also added some tinsel to make it sparkle. We only lit up the tree for a couple of nights. I am surprised we, or the other families, didn't burn down the apartment building. My mother loved to sing and we would sing along. The songs I remember singing were: Stillle Nacht (Silent Night); *Ihr kinderlein kommet* (Oh come, little children); and, *Leise rieselt der schnee still und starr liegt der se weihnachtlish glaauzed der wald, freuet euch das Kind Christus kommt* (How softly the snow falls on Christmas night, be joyful the Christ child is coming). When we were done with the tree, we hacked off all of the branches except the middle section, and made a potato masher. We wasted nothing, the cut off branches were thrown in the stove for heat.

When the big day came for the Carp feast, Ma would butcher the carp, scale it and bake it for the Christmas Eve meal. This was one of our biggest meals of the year for us. Ma saved up flour, carrots and potatoes to really make it special. My brothers and I would watch the preparations with great anticipation. It was really a treat. After the meal, we attended the Christmas Eve service as a family. This was one of the only times Ma went with us to church, at least until they boarded up all the churches.

We got our gifts on Christmas Day. We believed the Kriskindel, the Christ child, brought us gifts because it was his birthday. He was poorer than we were, so we didn't expect much. For Christmas presents we each would get a pencil or two, maybe a notebook and a stocking holder. The stocking holder was a harness similar to a garter belt that served to hold our long stockings up. Since we couldn't afford long pants, even in the winter, this helped us keep our legs warm. The gift exchange was always pretty lean, but we were content with whatever we got. I don't remember giving our ma anything but trouble, there just wasn't any money. This was a joyous family celebration despite the hard times.

This photo, dated 1941, was taken of my father while stationed in Paris. He is the second one from the left. He looks sad to have been forced to spend Christmas away from his family. The opulence of this gathering is in stark contrast to the humble celebration we enjoyed.

After the Christmas festivities, we hunkered down and rode out the winter, living one day at a time. We walked to and from school, half frozen most of the time. Sometimes we would hide in the ditch, wait for the horse drawn milk sled to pass and jump onto the back skis for a free ride. The milkman could feel our added weight and used his horse whip to snap us off after a short run. The whip had a sting, but it was nice to catch a bit of a free ride now and then in the frigid weather. If we were lucky we would dodge the whip by jumping off in time. We were always looking forward to spring for the warmer weather and to be able to get out and eat a little better.

We collected wood every year so we would have heat in the winter to subsidize the small amount of coal we were provided. We had a single wood stove in our one bed-room apartment. In the winter, it was so cold over night that even the milk would freeze. Thankfully, we had the feather blankets to keep warm through the night. It was just bad in the morning when you had to get out of bed. We had to get into our socks and shoes fast because our feet would freeze when they touched the floor. We didn't have much; so, we had to keep what we had a long time. We tried to keep warm so we wouldn't get pneumonia. No one would share food, clothes or wood to burn. Basically, it was everyone for themselves in the struggle to survive. The only exception was during the times I hung out with my gang and we all shared the fruits of our labor.

9

Easter Holiday

On Easter Sunday we also managed to visit the church as a family, but after church it was much better than Christmas. We each made a three foot long öster-peitsche, which was a whip-like object. We would cut long skinny willow reeds and weave them together like a pigtail to create the öster-peitsche. Then, on Easter Monday, we would visit mostly strangers, but also the most soft-hearted relatives we had, Tante Mitzi and her daughter, Meta. We would hit them with the whip if they gave their permission. In exchange, we received some small chocolate Easter Rabbits, candy or a shot of Brandy. After a few hours of this we had problems negotiating our way home. One time my small brother rolled down the river bank and I had a hell of a time rolling him back up and getting him to stand. You see, I was in no condition to carry him after at least seven shots of brandy. Brandy was much easier to acquire than chocolate, so that was our main payment. It was sort of like Halloween in America, well, except for the liquor. We called it schmeck-östern.

This is a photo taken of Ma and her three boys at a cousin's wedding in 1943. We got all dressed up for the occasion. I am 8 years old here, standing on the far right with the glint of mischief in my eye. I am right behind my obedient little brother who is 5 years old. At 11 years of age, my older brother is wearing an arm sling.

10

Life as a Scavenger

The other families who lived in our building had a father who remained with them. He was maybe too old or had a disability that kept him out of the army. All of us kids stuck together and were a regular bunch of scavengers. Of course we had our wars, we may have beaten each other up, but the next day we were friends again. We always shared amongst the group and had fun wherever we could find it. Finding food was a game. We never cried that we were hungry or poor; it was just a fact of life we dealt with so it just wasn't a big deal. We shared a bond that was forged by our environment and a need to be children despite the oppressive circumstances.

Of the gang I ran with, I had a real good friend named Rudy Geyer. His stepmother was known as "the witch." She had a big hooknose, not with a wart on it like a witch in a book, but she had a real screechy voice that was downright scary. The Geyer family had a couple of goats, so sometimes when I was over I would get a little goat milk, but very little. No one shared food, since they didn't have enough to spare. She kept goats in her wood shed and that provided their family with milk, cheese and eventually goat meat. Rudy was a classmate and he seemed rich to me because he had some toys. I would play at his house.

Rudy and I would take walks in the wood to gather certain leaves for the witch to make salve to be used on scrapes. The base of this salve came from pine trees branches that would be cut the week when the sap was running. Then we'd look for certain weeds the witch asked for, these weeds would be boiled with the pine sap. The resulting salve was stored in a stone crock and used as an antiseptic ointment. His stepmother would put home-made salve on my wounds if I asked nice. Once I had a stick from a cherry tree go through my foot when I landed on it jumping out of a tree I was raiding. This wound never got infected thanks to this salve.

My friend Leopold Habel lived right down the hall from me, we called him Poldy. He and I liked to play by the bridge built out of branches and manure where the horse carts would cross the river. One day while we were playing, Poldie dropped a log on my finger and squished it pretty bad. I had to go to Frau Geyer who looked at it, wiggled it and she told me it would be okay. It hurt but I recovered from it without any problems.

It really didn't take much for us to amuse ourselves.

LIFE AS A SCAVENGER

We played a little soccer and rolled a bicycle wheel for entertainment. Sometimes Rudy, Poldy and I would follow Frau Miller and spy on her. The Millers lived upstairs and they were pretty well off compared to us. Frau Miller had one leg shorter than the other and walked with a gimp. She was the camp whore. We always knew where she was going, so we could get there first and hide. She took her customers up to the dam. We watched as she hiked up her dress and the interested companion dropped his pants. When the action was over, she was paid with money, jewelry or food items. I guess it was natural curiosity for a bunch of young boys to watch, but we usually chose to spend our time on more useful pursuits.

Rudy, Poldy and I - along with the rest of the gang-fought turf wars with the gang from across the river. They called us "factory brats". Their swimming hole was upriver from ours, on the other side of the dam. At times we would try a sneak attack to raid their gardens. If they caught us it was war. We would throw clumps of dry clay at them. We would make swords from sticks we found at the saw mill and used them too. They really didn't need an excuse to start a fight, sometimes they were just in the mood to try to show off how tough they were. We had a secret weapon, though, Leopold's stupid older brother, Fred. He could take on two or three of them at one time. By the time it was over, we were all bloody, but went home feeling pretty proud of ourselves. It was entertainment for sure and definitely a way to blow off steam.

HANS

The gang had a system worked out to steal goose eggs from the farm down the road a bit. The girls would tease the German Shepherd guard dog, named Stift, with a stick through the fence to keep it busy while the boys slipped into the barn to swipe eggs. We would scoot the goose off of the nest by getting it mad. As the goose would chase the one guy and bite him in the ass, the other boys would quickly shake the eggs in the nest to find the good ones. We boys would also try to swipe some walnuts, cherries or pears off the trees while inside the fence...whatever was ripe at the time. We would give the trees a good shake and see what would drop off for a quick grab. We would all meet up at another spot to share our bounty. Using a sharpened stick, we would poke a hole in each end and suck the insides right out of the shell. Once in a while it was lumpy, but we didn't care. We never dared to take these eggs home because Ma would know they were stolen and we would catch heck for sure. One time Stift somehow got through the fence and Marianne, one of the girls, got tore up pretty bad. That Stift was a mean son of a bitch, but he was just doing his job. She went to the hospital for stitches, but recovered well enough with some scars to prove her valor. She was a good sport and kept running with us afterwards. We felt bad that she got chewed up, but it was part of the risk we each took to get food.

One of the gang's finest adventures ever happened on a sizzling summer day. We were out grazing in a farmer's field looking to eat some green cobs of corn, when we stumbled upon a secret garden planted by workers in the middle of the field. As far as we could tell, the farmer never knew about it. Wow, we thought we were in paradise. We were very smart about how we gathered the food out of this garden, though, and we took our time. We never left an open hole that would be obvious. Instead, we would pull individual carrots or kohlrabi spaced out along a row and then carefully covered up the holes. When we pulled off a cabbage head, we painstakingly arranged the outer leaves so it was not noticeable. The same process was done with cauliflower; we would pull a head and tie the leaves back up just how it had been. We did not want to ruin our personal pantry by alerting whoever planted it to a band of thieves. They still got a good crop out of it; it was just a bit lighter. We tucked our shirts into our pants and loaded the garden goods down our shirts. Then we took our feast to a secluded area, far from the field, and shared it. I remember smashing a head of cabbage and each of us just eating an eighth of the head raw. We were in absolute heaven as we crunched into the crisp treat and allowed the juice to dribble off our chins. Afterwards we just laid back and enjoyed the feeling of having a full stomach and friends to share it all with.

Seeking out food was the center of most of the gang's adventures but the key to success was having fun while doing it. We would go to the river and try to catch fish with our hands. It was fun to tease each other as we tried to land our slippery prey. Another time we collected a pile of small potatoes from various spots and burned them in a fire we made near the river. We all had black faces and teeth from eating the charred potatoes. We laughed as we cleaned ourselves up in the river before heading home.

We visited the British and Polish prisoners from time to time on our scouting trips. The flood plain near the river was full of willows and the prisoners had a work detail there under the supervision of the German guards. Their job was to reinforce the river dam by weaving willow branches together, 15-16 inches around, tied with wire and secured by wooden stakes. Eventually, the willows would take root and form a strong wall to create a secure flood barrier. The Polish prisoners made pretty carvings of birds out of the willows during their breaks. These birds looked pretty neat with intricate feathers, each carved individually. I was amazed to watch the prisoners create them. I once gave a prisoner a piece of bread in exchange for a bird and I kept that treasure on my dresser for a long time. The British prisoners were marched in to help build ammunition boxes at the factory where my father had worked. The prisoners didn't try to run away because I think there were treated pretty well. Mail and care packages were delivered to the British prisoners. One of the wonderful things they received in these boxes from Britain was candy. I got my very first chocolate bar in 1944 from a British POW. I put my hand through the fence and asked very politely for "chocolate" and I was handed a bar.

LIFE AS A SCAVENGER

To cool off on very hot days, our gang would go swimming bare in a swimming hole, both boys and girls, all about the same age. We hung our clothes on bushes and weren't a bit shy to see each other naked. We all slid down the clay banks, bare-assed, and splashed into the cool water below. It was a time filled with shrieks of laughter and silliness. We would have a pretty red hind end by the time we were done. We didn't care that we walked home sore, it was a slice of time to just be kids and forget our troubles.

One day Leopold didn't show up to play and I heard he was sick. His mother let me wave to him from the doorway but I wasn't allowed to get any closer. The next day they took him out dead. Leopold had died of diphtheria behind the doors of his apartment where a quarantine sign was posted. I remember seeing him being carried out in a sealed casket. I played with him up to two days before he died and I was very sad to lose a friend. I will never forget him, and looking back, I am thankful Poldy didn't suffer long. Already at that young age, I had come to understand that there were no guarantees in life and death was a mere whisper away.

11

My Small World View

My grades were good so I was allowed to attend the Oberschule (middle school). The boys went alone and the girls went alone so we were segregated. I was in the middle school for a total of five to six months and it was my first experience learning English. I was fascinated with the language and tried to soak up as much as I could in the short time I had.

The schools were closed when the air raids became frequent for fear the schools might get bombed. They also boarded up the churches so no one could attend services. After that I had no more school until years later in Bavaria. I focused all of my energy upon finding food and entertainment where possible.

I went to three meetings of the Hitler youth. They would talk politics the entire time and push the message that we were the future. I had to go to meetings to get prepared for it. The purpose of these meetings was to indoctrinate the youth by bragging up how good Hitler was for the German Reich. Meetings were held after school and each included the mandatory singing of "Deutschland über alles," which meant "Germany over all the world." Every voice joined in as we stood smartly at attention with our right arms raised.. No one dared to defy the ceremonious atmosphere of the meeting. I never got a uniform because you had to be ten years old. I never got a knife with a Swastika on it either. When I turned ten, the German military conquest was already going backward, they were getting their butt kicked and didn't want to admit it.

Many things were pounded into my brain at that time. Despite this overwhelming flood of information, there were countless details of which I had no idea. I never, ever knew that Jews were being put into camps. This was never mentioned in school or on the streets. I only had an idea about what was going on in my small corner of the world. People just disappeared and it could be anyone.

I was told by my mother to never talk against Hitler, not to utter a negative word about anything. If anyone would hear, they could report you and you would simply be "gone." I heeded her warning and witnessed first hand what terror ensued if someone was tattled on by an informer. With this mindset, everyone was tight-lipped, so I realized later how much could have been going on outside of the immediacy of my world. It was mandatory to greet everyone with "Heil Hitler." If anyone older passed you had to take your hat off, raise your arm and say, "Heil Hitler." It was just part of the game to survive.

12

Keeping an Eye to the Skies

In 1943, we had to block the windows with dark paper so the US air force flying overhead wouldn't know we were there. We had to put a black pull down shade in every window so we could have our lights on after dusk. It was required that we have these and we had to buy them. The punishment was severe if you were caught without a shade pulled down after dusk. Neighbors would turn each other in, so we never took the chance.

The American planes started flying over head bombing areas 30-50 miles away across the border in Poland, which were Beuten, Krussia, and Katowitz. The allies were helping to push the German troops out of Poland. By then, the US was bombing us pretty good. We would watch the action from the burg-burg. The burg-burg was the high point in town where the town watch tower was located. This was a perfect spot to watch the action. The Americans would drop bombs on factories. We were supposed to watch for parachutes but I never saw any. We were supposed to report any to the town so they could capture or shoot them. I wouldn't have anyway. I saw the Americans as a welcoming saving grace for my tattered existence. We could see the planes with the bomb doors open and knew a bomb would be tumbling out at any time. After a while we didn't worry about them anymore. At some point we just decided if we got hit, we got hit. It became an accepted part of life, just as the unsatisfied hunger that left the clothes hanging loose on our small frames.

The radio announced approaching enemy aircraft, but by the time they announced it the planes were already overhead. We knew what to do. We put the radio on the floor because this was our only source of information and it was essential to protect it. If a bomb hit too close there was a chance that the vibrations would shake the radio off the shelf and the tubes would be broken. The announcer would stay, "Posor, posor, dusch natz si vasa!" This was the warning which meant, "Attention, attention, this is important message!"

After safeguarding the radio, we'd run outside to watch the action. We would lie in a ditch and could see the anti aircraft puffballs that would come all around the plane. We watched as the planes changed heights to avoid the exploding shells from damaging their planes. Once in a while, we would see black smoke and we would know a plane got hit. It would break formation and head towards us. Now those were the ones that would really scare us because we didn't know where it would crash or drop a bomb. I think sometimes the pilots could spot us there in the ditch and made sure they didn't drop a bomb on us.

Our city was the biggest around with many textile factories, so they would try to target the industries. So, sometimes, they would go in too low and they would have to drop the bomb in the outskirts. When the bombs came out of the plane they would tumble, we weren't too worried when we could see them tumbling because they would hit a ways away, but we got worried when we saw the planes coming with the door open. We were lucky. The closest bomb was dropped 100-150 yards away from us. We used the crater made by this bomb as a swimming hole. One plane dropped a spare fuel tank over us and that was a wonderful gift. We chipped that out and made a boat to float down the river. Someone stole it from us, though, I had a feeling it was the gang across the river.

The end of 1944 marked a sense of desperation on the part of Germany's war machine. The age to be drafted was lowered to sixteen in order to bolster the number of troops. I was not old enough at age ten to be drafted, but I watched the dwindling of able-bodied men in our area. Those left behind included older or disabled men and boys aged 15 or younger. This pretty much included me and my gang of renegade children scouring the countryside for food

Things kept getting worse, and the planes started coming more often. Over the German radio, we kept hearing that we were still winning, but we knew better. It was getting worse. It did not take long for the distant cannons to be heard and the rumble of artillery, the planes kept coming. Next, the Germans starting digging fox holes near us, in the dam, because we had floods and the dam was built to keep us dry. They supervised a work detail of Polish prisoners to build really nice foxholes hollowed out of the dam. The workers then covered each fox hole with boards and grass so it couldn't be detected from above by the airplanes. They made slits in the front so the soldiers could shoot out, yet be protected from enemy fire. Burlap covered the foxholes from behind so they were camouflaged.

After watching the preparations underway, we decided it would be wise to be prepared ourselves. We found a location under a willow tree near our house and dug a hole. We lined it with boards and tar paper to prevent the contents from getting wet. In it, we buried the few things of value that we had. This included linen, silverware and a few trinkets Ma had. We put boards, tar paper and grass over top to hide it. It was important because we needed to save some of our things until the hoarding was over. Someone must have been watching us, though, because all of these items were stolen.

By early 1945, the Allies controlled the air and the Germans were being systematically bombed in the air and on the ground. The RAF Bomber Command, along with the U.S. Air Force under the command of General Doolittle, "were able to roam the German skies with near impunity" (Jablonski, 1977, pg. 256). The Allied Air Force deftly evaded flak from anti-aircraft ground defenses as they successfully completed bombing missions by day and night. According to Jablonski (1977), the air dominance of the Allies served to punctuate the end of Germany's "Fourth Front" (the air) and Hitler's secret weapon, the Messerschmitt 262, was never effectively used as a weapon against the American bombers.

The food supply got to be even scarcer at this point; we had stamps and some money but there was no food available to buy with it. My little brother and I would stand in line for hours for potatoes or horsemeat, but there was only so much available. When they ran out, the message was, "That's just tough, better luck next time." Slowly we got used to being hungry. We butchered all of our rabbits and a couple chickens that we had left. We ate them before someone else did. Then we started to look for dogs and cats, there were not many around because no one had food. When we would find one, we did the best we could to skin it out and have a feast. I think the owner of the butcher shop saw us coming and left out some sausage casings on the window sill. We would reach up to grab these tasty ends, then run and eat them. We basically kicked into a heightened level of survival mode at this point.

13

Memories of my Soldier Father

After he was drafted in 1939, my father came home once a year on vacation. First he was stationed in Germany, and then he joined the Medic-core where he was trained to do basic medical care. He got transferred to Paris after a year and a half while France was occupied by the Germans. My father sent my ma letters and occasionally included a photo.

This photo was taken in 1942 after my father completed medical training in Paris, France. The arrow is pointing to my father. Note the ominous picture of Hitler centered in the shot. I can't help but wonder how many of these men were also forced to serve and took the high road as medics.

HANS

After his stint in France, he was sent to Athens, Greece. I never saw much of him when he was home on leave. My parents would sometimes go to a movie together while I stayed home with my brothers. The time with my father home always went quickly. He would visit with other family members and we stayed home. These short spans of time were punctuated by bittersweet memories of a man I never truly had the chance to know.

On one visit, he came home with a new patch on his uniform. He had been promoted to a sergeant. He was still in the medical core in the air force. He really looked decked out in his uniform. Even though he was a German soldier, I always knew he hated Hitler. We were taught to strictly follow the rules because the SS was the enforcer. People would disappear all of the time. It was my father's biggest fear that we would all be shot while he was forced to be away from home and too far away to protect us.

This is my father's photo taken after his promotion to Air force Sergeant while stationed in Athens, Greece. It is dated 1944

MEMORIES OF MY SOLDIER FATHER

I found out much later how often he really thought about us back at home. He and my mother exchanged letters regularly to stay in touch. At least they did until my father screwed up and pissed Ma off. The last time he was home my mother became angry with him after finding a love note tucked into his sleeve from a young woman, a stranger from another country. We could hear the shouting and knew Ma accused him of being with another woman. He claimed that Ma was the love of his life, and insisted that no other woman mattered to him. Despite hearing this testimony of love, Ma was both hurt and angry at him.

Thinking back on it, I guess I don't blame her for being infuriated. She was stuck watching the three of us and working long hours in the factory while worrying about his safety and then she finds out he was having a romantic fling. I also can't really blame my father. He was far from home and not sure which day would be his last. Now that I know he died young, I am glad that he was able to find comfort and companionship in his life. Desperate times present a different spin on life and I refuse to judge him. I do wonder, however, if I have any half brothers or sisters running around in another country.

HANS

My father is located on the far right next to the poor sap with the bandaged leg. This photo was taken while he was stationed in Athens, dated 1944. He looks like he is enjoying some down time with his comrades. Perhaps the hint of the war finally coming to a close served to lighten the mood.

Despite how upset she was, Ma begged him not to return to the front that last time. He told us that the Germans were losing and were on the run. That last long goodbye was an emotional mixture of hope that it was almost over and fear that we would never see each other again. My ma had an added dread of losing the love of her husband as he climbed aboard the train taking him back to Greece. He told my mother that Germany had lost the war and that it would not go very far, anymore. My mother pleaded with him to stay home, that we would go into hiding. But he said that if he didn't report back in time, he would be marked as a defector and the SS death squad would come shoot us all. He said that as soon as it started going the other way he would try to get away. He promised to come back and said a final farewell. That was the last time I saw my father.

The last letter my mother received from my father

was kept folded in her pocket most of the remainder of her life. She read and reread that final message but kept its contents private. It wasn't until years after her death that I unfolded the fragile yellowed communiqué and read it myself. The following is my English translation of the words he penned by his own hand in our native German language approximately one month before he was killed:

1945, February 14   *Write soon!*

My dearest Wife! In the beginning I say a quiet servus my dear and hereby I will many times to my heart and give you thousands of Kisses, my only one on this world, also many kisses for the 3 well behaved Boys. It's been 4 weeks since I left you all. How time Flies. Soon another year is gone. I wished to be able to look into the Future, what will be happening? so that all this War is not for nothing. I only have one Wish- that my Homeland is safe from the Russians and you my dear Family will be safe and all remain Healthy. I am waiting each day with great hope to receive a letter from you. I can't relax thinking of you all, especially in the evening before I go to sleep. I am thinking of you, what you are doing right now, at the same Time when I think of you.

We just got done waiting 14 hours for a Guerrilla attack and I was happy that we are heading North-West, we only had a few Kilometers for our planned destination but there was a change of orders so we had to go back from where we started the previous Day.

If you could only see, when the Lanzers Guerrillas are attacking, you would really laugh. They are coming 5 or 6 on 3 small sleds. When we had more snow, they were hooked up to a Horse being pulled, it looked like our children on their small sleds used at Home. Then if they hit the horse and it runs, a lot of times they fell off and rolled into the soup; or Ditch when they get to a turn in the Road. Then some jumped on horses without saddles an, if the Horse stumbles, the Proud Rider comes face down into the mud. I also fell from our wagon, when we retreated, because there was so much mud and bad roads full of Holes. I was mud from head to Toe but I had to get back up and we continued our Retreat after I got back up on the Wagon and the Horses kept on going. Since it was all mud, I could not get hurt by the Fall. Now we have very little Snow, mostly mud and water and it even runs into the top of our Boots because it is only Flatland we are on right now. Otherwise we live good. If we are on the move, we stop for one hour and a few of us go into small Farm houses to eat a meal, even if there is no one home. There is always White Bread and Pork-back fat (Speck) in the smallest Houses and most of the time Wine which is very important here. Now you can see how well I am taking care of myself-- I turned out to be a real Gypsy. Every day, somewhere else, but it is beautiful besides all of the hardships, my Dear. You know I always had a fine Nose for finding a safe place to set up my overnight camp. Now my Dear, I want to close for Today. All the intimate greetings and Kisses, many Thousand Times in intimate Love.

Your Husband, Guste

(This was written along the margin: *Many Dear Greetings to Rudi, Hedwig, Meta, Herr Tukerneck and all Relatives and Friends.)*

This is the last solitary photo that I have of my father. It was taken in 1944 while he was stationed in Athens, Greece. It was from this location that he and his unit were ordered to retreat. He looks relaxed and happy here...just how I want to remember him.

I turned eleven that year and I waited for a long time to see my father return as he had promised. I knew he sacrificed his dreams, his freedom, and possibly his life to keep his family from being killed. It was an unselfish choice and the greatest gift he gave me. He taught me, through his actions, that there are hard choices a man must make in life. It was many years later, after we had been in America for two to three years, that we discovered he was killed by snipers in Greece when his battalion was ambushed by Partisans. An Austrian witness, a survivor of the attack, confirmed that my father was among the dead. Up to that time he was considered missing in action. We never had the chance to say goodbye or give him a proper burial or even know where he was buried. He has lived on within me, though, a whisp of a childhood memory wrapped in both reverence and regret that I was cheated of really knowing my father.

At that time, I drew upon my determination to keep going in hopes that our family would someday be whole again. My younger brother was at my side, following my lead. I watched out for him and we shared a bond like no other person in my life. My mother continued to work long days in the clothing factory and my older brother went his own way with his friends, so that left the two of us to our own devices for the better part of each day. At times we ran with the gang, and other times we ran alone. It was the game of survival with loose rules, but one rule that was never broken was brothers watching each other's back so we would make it to see another day.

My mother and older brother always thought we had rich friends that gave us food, but we really stole it. For some reason, I never bonded with my older brother. He ate what was on the table but didn't help to provide, we gave up on his help. He hung around with buddies his own age and he never really told us what he did all day. My younger brother and I had a perfect system worked out. We were very observant as we scoped out the town's gardens which were each guarded by a fence and the watchful eyes of the owner. I would carry a stick to pry the tenth fence board from one corner of the fenced garden and the eighth from the other. We were skinny enough that if our head fit through, the rest of our bodies would follow. One of us would be a decoy in case we were caught. The only time Ma found out was when we had raided the cherry trees. The cherries were loaded in our shirts and the farmer grabbed my leg, pulling me out of the tree. He slapped me across the face each way and then yelled for my brother to get out of the tree. He cried that he was too scared to crawl down, while the owner was crawling up the tree to get him down; I took off running toward the fence post I knew would be loose. When I got close to the fence post, I made some noise to get the attention of the owner. When he looked my way, he got out of the tree to chase me. Then my brother dropped out of the tree and ran the other direction to our other loose fence post. We got through the fence so fast that the cherries smashed and juice was running down our shorts. We didn't get caught by the farmer, but we got the crap beat out of us by our ma because we couldn't wash the red stains out of our shirts or pants.

HANS

We both knew all the orchards and had it planned out so we always had an alternate escape route just in case we got caught. The orchards were pretty well protected by fence and barbed wire. We would scout it out ahead of time and work a fence post loose so we could slip through. One day we were up in the trees picking cherries and the farmer yelled at us to come down out of the tree. I could run faster, being older, so I gave my little brother a head start by keeping the farmer busy with me. I faked a twisted ankle to distract him and when my brother was in the clear, I ran the other direction and slipped between the loosened fencepost. The farmer didn't catch us but he yelled quite loud and we avoided that orchard for a while. We planned our raids carefully; it was a way to get some food and was also a game to us. We avoided being shot at a number of times using this strategy. I feel that my father would have been proud of his sons.

14

A Changing of the Guard

Not long afterwards, I think about April, the cannons were hitting. We could see the dirt fly in the distance. The Germans were on the run. They didn't even stop to take up position in the nice foxholes that were dug and stocked with ammunition, machine guns, and hand grenades. They just headed out and went by us without taking up a position to fight. I don't know if they had orders to retreat or just headed out on their own. They had created sophisticated land mines, something like an upside-down mouse trap, on their way to stop the advance of the Russians. These traps were created by knocking down light poles to form a barricade between the houses. The Germans built up mounds of cobblestones, shored up by the light poles, with the land mines positioned below the rocks. That way, if the poles were moved, the quartz stones would tumble away to release the pressure trigger. The blast would then blow up the Russians soldiers or tanks.

We decided it might be a good time to leave too, with the Russians coming. It made sense that the Russians would probably shoot everything up since they would plan on leaving a path of destruction in their wake. We didn't have many options to seek refuge, so we headed to my mother's sister's house about twelve miles away from Jägerndorf. In preparation for leaving the apartment, we buried all the stuff that was half ways decent in the hole that we had made before and covered it real good with board and dirt to make it look natural. We figured everything left behind in the apartment would be stolen. In a little wagon, we put the heavy stuff and each of us carried a little backpack. Then we went to see Aunt Hilda who lived in Erbersdorf. Her husband did not want us there. He was a real stubborn asshole. My aunt begged him to allow us to stay and argued with him. We stood at their front door with our little wagon, watching them fight it out. He finally gave in with a stern warning - if we made any noise or any trouble, out we go!

My uncle commanded my aunt, "No food for them." He even counted the ripe tomatoes in the garden and promised to beat us if we ate any. So, we picked green ones. Of course he spotted us chewing. After he had forced our mouths open to see what we were eating, we got a good beating. After that we went out to find our own food which was no problem because we were used to it.

A CHANGING OF THE GUARD

The barefooted brothers continued the search for food in a new area. The Germans had a field station with a bakery not far away; it was just outside of town. We hung around there to do odd jobs. There were horses and a shipping area where they sent supplies to the front. We cleaned the horses and for that we would get a loaf of bread or a piece of meat or sausage. We scouted out that they had a big stack of 100-kilo bags of flour. So my brother and I thought it would be a good thing to keep our eye on it. One day after all of the Germans were gone, we checked out the field station. Sure enough, there were a couple bags of flour left behind. They couldn't take it all in their haste to outrun the Russians. We pulled out the stakes holding it in place, and managed to pull one bag 50-60 feet to a ditch. We carefully hid it under some grass and made plans to return for it later.

By the time we got back from hiding the flour, the shooting was starting and there were a few straggler soldiers coming. They were blowing up a bridge near there in an effort to stop the Russians. We spotted a Cossack riding in. We saw this wild looking guy riding into the city on a small scraggly horse. We quickly ran behind the bushes while we kept an eye on him. We noticed that he had spotted a young woman there on the side of the road. He jumped off his horse and pulled her into the ditch. We knew what was going on there; she just didn't have a chance and no one dared to help her. We just kept quiet and hid.

HANS

After he finished raping the girl, he got back on his pony and paraded into town. He yelled something in Russian, probably about seeing the mayor or someone in charge of the village. Finally, someone could understand part of it and explained to him that we would not resist. He rode back out and it didn't take long and a wild bunch of Russians and Mongols came into town. This wild bunch looked mean and dirty. After they were done scouting out the town, they moved on to the next town.

After the first dirty bunch went through, the next Russians that came were a little better dressed with clean uniforms and shiny polished boots. They weren't as bad, but we had no idea who was coming down the road next. It was a very unsettling feeling. They took over the building where the Germans had had the bakery and made it a temporary headquarters. They methodically went into all the houses on a sweep of the city. They were looking for money and livestock to confiscate. One commissar with two other soldiers came into my aunt's house. My mother and her sister, with her husband, were standing there when these three entered the house; we children were all scared and hiding in the corner. They pointed their sub-machine guns at all of us as a warning to keep us quiet. The Russians had a round cylinder attached to their guns to feed in the ammo, unlike the Germans who had a straight ammunition clip. Then, the commissar grabbed my mother and pulled her up the stairs, she cried out a couple times but we could not get away to help her. We knew what was happening upstairs and were terrified for our mother, but again we felt helpless to change the course of events.

About twenty minutes later, he came down alone. My uncle was waving his arms trying to tell him something and the commissar saw his watch and wanted it. My uncle tried to talk him out of it, not wanting to give up his watch. The soldiers gave my uncle the butt of the gun in his face and there was blood flying all over the place from his newly missing teeth. So, he finally gave him the watch. We were still huddled in the corner; the soldiers pointed their guns at us again before they went out the door. After that initial meeting, they would come back once in a while to see if we had any food or anything worth taking with them before they eventually moved on.

I couldn't help but wonder what was going on with our gang and if our apartment building was still standing. My little brother and I talked about it and decided to take a look for ourselves. With this decision made, we agreed to leave secretly early the next morning. I don't know how we managed it, but we got that little wagon and went to the ditch, and oh boy, there was our bag of flour. We tugged and pulled and somehow got it into the wagon, it weighed about 100 kilos. Then we put branches over it to hide it in the wagon. We headed back along the road and it was a gruesome sight. We saw dead cattle and smelled the decaying carcasses as we tugged our load along the bumpy road. What a waste to see all of that rotting food when we were so hungry. There were also dead

HANS

German soldiers all bloated up, left to lie were they fell as the Russians swept through the countryside. The soldier's uniforms were stretched tight, with the buttons ready to pop off, because the bodies were so bloated up. We didn't dare go near the bodies because we were afraid that someone would think that we were trying to take something and they would shoot us.

We kept marching on, purposefully, undaunted by the carnage littering the road and the smell of death hovering like a fog. We knew the route quite well since it was the main road back to Jägerndorf. We pulled our precious cargo past familiar houses. Now and then we could see raggedy faces in the windows looking out at us. No one offered us any food or water and we didn't dare ask. We just stopped to drink water out of the ditch every once in a while and kept going. When my little brother couldn't keep up, I would have him sit on the wagon so he could rest his legs. It was a hilly route, so I would steer the wagon down the inclines as my brother hopped on for the ride. Our goal was to get the flour back home to hide it before someone took it away from us.

By nightfall we made it back to our house. The first thing we did was hide the flour in the wood shed where we used to have the rabbit. We put straw over it, way back in the corner, we thought we would spend one night in our house and in the morning we would head out. We just got settled in when we heard shouting in Russian and the splintering noise of doors breaking. We peeked out into the hall and saw some Mongols and dirty Russians looking for valuables or food in our house. We really got scared, locked the door, and jumped out the window. We hid just below the window, flattening ourselves against the outside wall. One Mongol stuck his head out and looked around, but didn't see us. After he pulled his head in, we ran, scrambling silently into the darkness on our bare feet.

We decided it was time to head back to my Aunt's village. So, we snagged our wagon from the shed and headed on down the road. We made it about half way back when we were surprised by a Russian with a gun. He told us to stop. It was my fault that we were captured. I had stopped to check the identification on some bloated German soldiers who had their heads split open. There were three or four of them that looked like they were hit with a hatchet and flies were all over their brains. I was distracted and horrified by the sight of it. I heard someone say, "Rucki Wech," which means "put your hands up over your heads." When I raised my arms and turned, there was a Russian pointing a gun at me. He was only six feet away and must have snuck up on us. He took my brother and me along with him to take care of milking the cows they had stolen, so we could make cream. I managed to kick our little wagon into the ditch before we followed him. The Russians didn't keep prisoners at that time; they would just kill people and keep moving. They must have figured a couple of skinny boys would be good for doing chores and they could smuggle us back into Russia. We stuck with them until we got further away.

They had taken cows from a neighboring village; they had about seven cows, and a cream separator that they probably took from the cheese factory. So, they pointed to us that we had to stay and take care of the cows for them. We were supposed to milk them and run it through the separator so they would have cream to drink. We were starved and real skinny, so it was a special treat for us to think of getting milk, we were in bad shape by that time. We decided to make them happy and stay to take care of the cows while we drank all the milk we could.

Of course the Russians were drinking Vodka all night, so we all got started late the next day. They pointed east and we knew they were headed back towards Russia. We knew the area quite well from collecting wood and going mushroom hunting, so we knew where we were even though it was a couple miles from town. For three days we were with them and did as we were shown to do. I told my brother to just laugh and act like we were happy to be going to Russia. It worked because they didn't bother tying us up and treated us well. Then a smiling Russian came over and gave us a shot of Vodka and a chunk of pressed dried liver. This must have been their combat rations. It was a win-win situation and we decided to use it to our advantage

We got a little ways into Poland with this traveling Russian troop, when we decided to fly the coop before we got too far. We still knew about where we were and felt confident that we could find our way back. So that night we drank all the milk we could and left them a nice present by urinating in the can of cream before we left. There were three gallons or so in the can when we made our deposit. We also ate a chunk of liver while we waited for the Russians to all get drunk which was their normal evening activity. They played music on a bellenka, a type of mandolin, and were having a grand time. Our hosts were dancing and singing as we quietly slipped into the night. We departed in peace and headed back toward home. When we got back to where we began this little detour, the soldier bodies were gone -someone must have buried them - but our little wagon was still there.

We collected the wagon out of the ditch and quickly made our way back to our aunt's house. We did not stop to sight see this time, no matter how interesting the scenery was. Upon our arrival, Ma was nearly hysterical with joy, relief and anger. She asked what happened to us. She had thought we were killed or that they had taken us away. We told her we had taken the flour to hide and she gave us a good beating because we weren't supposed to do that. I left out the part about the Russians kidnapping us because that would have given her a reason to beat on us some more.

Our uncle had recovered enough by that time to get nasty with us. He took it out on us that he lost his teeth and his watch to the Russians. My uncle was bad tempered and staying in the same house with him was very tense. We all knew we were unwelcome guests.

My ma sat us down and discussed the situation with us. As a single mother, she had few options to offer. We all decided that it couldn't be any worse back in Jägerndorf. A bonus was that we wouldn't have to put up with our uncle there. So, we packed up our meager belongings, grabbed the wagon, and headed back down the now familiar road to our home.

The biggest thing we noticed upon our arrival back to Jägerndorf was that there weren't many people left in town. After the Russian drive, townspeople started to drift back from different quarters and holes. We had a bakery that was operational and that was a good sight. The churches remained boarded up and the only operational school was that of the real-life lessons learned on the streets. It seemed as though an air of watchful waiting was left in the wake of the Russian surge. The citizenry appeared to be waiting for the other shoe to drop, knowing we weren't totally in the clear.

Upon our arrival back at our apartment complex, my little brother and I went to check on our bag of flour. We were disappointed to discover it was gone. I wrote it off to scavengers and almost forgot about it until I noticed it stashed in the closet at Rudy's apartment a few days later. Frau Geyer, Rudy's step-mom, had taken our big bag of flour. I knew it was the same one my brother and I dragged in our little wagon because of the scuffs on the bag. She must have watched us hide it in the wood shed and dragged it up to her apartment when we ran from the Mongrels. Now that was an unwritten violation of our community trust, so I told Ma about it. She marched right up to the apartment and boy was there a fight. I was really proud of Ma. She demanded the flour back and that's when the fight started. Sometime during the scuffle, Ma ended up giving the witch a black eye when she refused to return the flour. After all of the punching, pushing, screaming and hair pulling was over, the two brawlers finally compromised on splitting the flour We returned to our apartment triumphant with our prized portion of hard earned flour.

With the Germans on the run and the Russians claiming victory, the atmosphere in town changed. At that time there were many Czechs and Jews that had been laying low, now taking over possession of the city. They boldly laid claim to all of the nice houses in town. They just picked a house and moved in. If there was anyone living there, they were evicted. Instead of maintaining order by preventing this blatant theft, the police enforced this shift of ownership. Quietly, the scales of power transferred from those obedient to the Germans to the new power players in town- the Russians, Czechs and Jews.

One day the police came to our home and announced that we were now considered prisoners. As prisoners we could be outdoors, but we had to sew a white tag three inches wide and six inches long and pin an "N" on it ten centimeters high so people would know we were "Nemski." Being marked this way, people could spit on us and beat us if they could catch us, but not many could. So, whenever we walked to town to buy bread or anything, we would avoid the older boys emboldened to attack us. They would be after us to beat us up so we had to be smarter and quicker than they were. This added a whole new dimension to the game of survival. We had to find food and get it home while successfully dodging others intending to hurt us. It seemed that we were always the losers and misfits; this was just another example of it. We couldn't reason out what we had done to be treated this way. Once again, we were defenseless to change things, so we made the best of it and took one day at a time.

There was much suspicion and unrest during this time period. It was difficult to sort out the bad guys from the good guys, or what side anybody was on. It seemed as though the tables were turned and many people felt emboldened to not only voice opinions, but act on them. They wanted to get into the good graces of the Russians and Czechs, so it was a virtual free-for-all with neighbors ratting out neighbors, even with half-truths. While we were happy that Hitler looked like he would be defeated, we were not so happy about those running the new game in town. They were terrifying in their own self-righteousness.

The killing continued, only the killers had changed. The landlord of the apartment building was caught trying to blow up some machinery so the Russians couldn't use it. They caught him as he was setting the charges and shot

him on the spot. The farmer across the street was shot
and killed by the Russians. He was a nice guy who gave
ma a job picking potatoes and stuffing straw in exchange
for some tallow or bones. Max Widra, the owner of the
farm, would also butcher animals from his farm to share
with the families when things were really tight and many
were starving. The Russians wanted to take his farm, so
he was shot.

On one such foraging mission, my brother and I witnessed an appalling sight. The route we took went past
the barricade built by the Germans to prevent tanks from
crossing the river into town. The barricade had been built
by placing wood planks over the cobblestone bridge with
land mines inside designed to blow the treads off of the
tanks. As we walked past, we noticed there was a Catholic priest laboring along side nine or ten men. They were
working to pull the barricade out so the Russians could
use the bridge. We tried to walk up to talk to them, but
the Russian guards supervising the work chased us off. We
weren't far off when one of those landmines exploded.
We spun around to look back toward the bridge and saw
that the priest was crumpled in a heap, looking like he got
hurt pretty bad. The others men were lying nearby on the
ground bleeding. We wanted to help, so we headed back
toward the river. The Russians saw us and pointed a gun
at us. They brusquely told us to get away or else. We took
the hint and went back to town. We continued on our trip
looking for food. We kept our eyes peeled for something

like a dog or cat, anything would do. Since we couldn't find any food, we gave up and retraced our steps. When we walked back past that spot on the bridge some time later there was just blood stains left. The people were gone and we didn't know what they did with them. We just kept heading for home and minded our own business.

We headed home and, still hungry and empty hand-ed, we decided to do a little fishing. We had an awful lot of luggers, pistols and hand grenades that we had found in deserted fox holes when the Germans retreated. We had lots of ammunition that we had hidden among the rocks. A Polish guard was by the river. We were worried that he would stop us. So we built a fire and put about 50 rounds of ammunition into it that we had gotten from the Germans. We hid behind the bank, when those things went off he came running with his tommy gun, he thought someone was trying to invade Poland. When he got close we jumped up and waved our arms and shouted and pointed and shouted, "Bang, bang, bang!" He understood and seemed like a good guy, and went on to do his rounds. When he was a couple hundred yards away, we dropped two hand grenades into the water after we pulled the pin together, and holy cow, there were a couple of nice white fish floating up. We looked at the guard to see if he would come back, but he just turned and waved at us. He thought we were playing another prank on him so he left us alone. We got to know that guard pretty well, and would return with hand grenades to get more fish, time and time again. We had river fish dinners and food in our stomachs.

For a time we were holding our own; but, things didn't go like that for long. I had thought we had hit bottom and things could only get better. Little did I know that life was going to throw us another curve ball, and this one almost took us out of the game.

15

Paybacks are Hell

One day in early May, with no prior warning, a guy with a Jewish armband came to the door. A couple of Czechs were standing behind him and looked like tough guys. They told us we had to go to a camp to register so they would know who we were. We were given the option to stay in our apartment, but we would have to agree to become Czechs and fall under communist rule. If not, we were to report to the camp. From the camp, we were promised to have a chance to go to Bavaria and a start a new life. Ma didn't hesitate; she firmly stated our family did not want to be Czech. They told us to take any valuables with us because there were many thieves around. They stood and watched as we gathered our belongings. My mother put her valuables in her bag, and hung a leather sack around her neck with all her savings in it. We each carried a bag with some clothes for a couple days and some blankets. They told us we would only be gone a couple of days and promised us we would be safe. I was suspicious of our escorts and felt very uneasy about how things might turn out. In a short time, like a pack of gypsies, we once again were heading down a road with no clear destination.

I don't know how far we walked, but we finally reached the camp. When we got to the gate, we realized it was an old German army camp reinforced with barbed wire. I quickly scanned the area and noticed guards with machine guns standing in the guard towers. Following directions, we checked in near the gate. This area had long tables set up with men sitting there. Guards were standing behind the men with their guns pointed at us. They said that we had to give them anything of value or anything that could be used like a weapon. They confiscated guns, knives, and scissors from people moving through the line. We had no choice; we were told that this was the end of the line and we'd better cooperate or it would go badly for us. We handed over the few valuables we owned. My mother cried when she gave them the leather pouch, it represented all of her savings. I was shocked when she told me later that she had saved five thousand pounds. Unbeknownst to us kids, she had been scraping by all of these years to save for a home to buy after the war was over and pa returned.

The Jews stationed at the registration table said they would give our valuables back when we left, but we never saw our things again. My mother didn't want to give them her wedding ring. They tried to pull it off but they couldn't get it off her finger, so they left it. I will never forget how these particular Jews looked. They were healthy looking, wearing nice long black coats adorned with the yellow Jewish Star like a badge of honor. Their hair was done up with perfect spit curls. The way they looked, smug and with more meat on their bones than we had, I later decided that these guys never could have spent time in a camp. We later figured they took the riches they collected from the German residents as some sort of pay back for sins of which we were ignorant of. At the time, I had no clue what was going on or why.

After taking our meager treasures and any possible weapons, the armed guards marched us to the barracks. There was not much inside; no beds to sleep on, just a bare floor. We took a look around and we hoped we would only be there a couple of nights. We picked a spot and spread our blankets on the floor. More people kept coming and the room soon filled up.

That night a whistle blew and we had to go outside and line up. The guards told us we would get one meal a day because there wasn't much food. Again, we were told that we would get out in a couple days. We all stood in line to get a half tin-cup of hot water with a couple potatoes peels in it. That was our soup. There was no salt in it because of a salt shortage there and of course, no meat.. We also would get a half slice of rye bread with a little piece of cheese. They said that was it, and, well it turned out that was our daily meal for the next five or six months. I'm not sure how long we were there...it seemed like it was forever but I didn't have a calendar to go by to know exactly.

I distinctly remember that they thinned us out on the second day. We all got marched outside and lined up for inspection. All the men and boys over fourteen got separated out of the crowd. I was thinking they did this so they wouldn't give them any trouble. These prisoners got sent to a separate area of the camp, and, later in the day, they were escorted to an unknown destination. As they were marched out of camp there was a rumor that they were being taken away to Siberia, never to be seen again. We think they may have been sent away to a work camp, but we never knew for sure because they did not come back. After that, all that was left in camp were older men, women, and children up to 13 years of age. My older brother was so sickly and scrawny; they rejected him from being sent away because he looked younger. Although he would have been about 15 years old they couldn't prove his age.

It was very dark in the barracks after dusk. With no electricity, we sat or laid in total darkness after the sun went down. Mothers tried to soothe their frightened children the best they could, but comfort measures were limited. While staring into the blackness on the second night, I heard the guards enter the barracks. They came to pull out the women and young girls, I couldn't see them but I knew this was happening from the noise and commotion. I could hear their screams- begging for mercy that was not granted – that echoed through the night. I knew they were being raped as we lay in darkness; once again I felt helpless to stop the brutality. The only ones left to defend their honor was a bunch of dispirited old folks, young boys and very young girls. The guards brought them back when they were done with them, like it was their right to use them like animals for their own pleasure.

After that night, most of the mothers would try to make their young girls look dirty, and stinky, just so they would leave them alone. I think most of them got taken out anyway, despite the mothers' efforts to protect them. It became an expected, unspeakable horror which, during the daylight, no one discussed. Night fall was met with a sense of dread on the ensuing evenings. My stomach turned in knots as I silently awaited the inevitable nocturnal visitors, the whimpering struggles against wickedness and the ongoing destruction of innocence.

The only one of my gang that made it to this camp with me was my buddy Rudy Geyer. His dad was among those sent to Siberia or a work camp; and his mother died there in the camp a few days later. I pleaded with my Ma to help Rudy. My mother tried to pretend he was my brother so he could join our family, but someone squealed on us. They dragged Rudy away before my eyes and all I could do was wave a silent farewell to my friend as I choked back the tears. I never saw him again. To this day, I wonder what happened to one of my best buddies.

As time passed and the callus around my heart thickened, I got used to basic camp life just as I had with every other obstacle thrown my way. As a group, we were allowed out of the barracks to get soup with the sound of the whistle. We were trained like animals...whenever the whistle blew we left the barracks to line up. An old wagon rolled into the camp, with a big make shift soup kettle on it. This wagon had a route between various camps and work sites. We were so hungry that we looked forward to the once a day ritual. We continued to get a cup of the watery excuse for soup, a half piece of bread and a quarter size piece of cheese. We had to take care of the cup we were given. If it was lost, we could not get any soup. After three to four weeks, I remember not being hungry anymore.

The Jews walked around camp with their long black coats adorned with a yellow Jewish star. They were mostly there to supervise and seemed to take pleasure in our deplorable conditions. The camp was mostly run by Jews, Russian guards and there was a Commissar overseeing the operations.

As the weeks wore on, our hair was shorn off due to head lice. Our blankets were teeming with bed bugs and we had bites all over our emaciated bodies. To counter the infestation, we were forced to walk through the delousing spray once a week. Since we were sent back to the same infested bedding it didn't help anything. The caustic spray smelled horrible. It stung my nose, making me cough and gag as I endured the weekly ritual. The stench of it clung to my skin and continued to assault my senses for days. It was another miserable experience to add in to an all around hellish episode in my life.

One night there was an assembly arranged. When we were all marched out, there was about half of a football field filled with people. No one knew why we were congregated there. The guards dragged out one guy and started to beat him in front of everyone. Someone had squealed on him that he had something to do with the German Reich. We were forced to watch as the beating and berating continued. Anyone who looked away would get a stern warning to watch the action or else it could be them next. The guards only stopped when the beaten man quit screaming and became unconscious. Then we all got marched back to the barracks. We never knew if the beaten prisoner was dead or killed after we left. We were not given an explanation, but the demonstration sent a clear message to not resist their authority. After that, not every night, but two to three times a week they would find someone else to beat. This appeared to be both our instructional demonstration and entertainment for our captors. I don't know how many people died in the camp, but we saw wagons being taken out that looked to be laden with bodies.

The time stretched on, hour by hour, day by day, and

we lived each of them with the hope of surviving to find a better life. We existed amidst despair, anger and fear of the unknown. We overcame the anguish that threatened to destroy us by keeping alive a faith focused upon a better future. This one thing carried me through the darkest times.

My mother's sister, one of the rotten relatives, was in the camp with us also. Tante Headrick continuously tried to talk our mother into killing herself to end the misery. She insisted that it could not continue; that it would be better to be dead than live this way. After listening to her endless wailing, I finally stepped in and told her to just kill herself and leave us alone. We- the three brothers and Ma- resolved to try to make it. She stopped talking that way to my mother after that. Some people hung themselves and did commit suicide, but she never did.

After a couple of weeks, the guards started marching my mother and older brother out through the gates in the morning with the other women and older children. I lived with the secret dread that they might never come back. I would watch for their return and was relieved when they were marched back to camp at the end of the day. The soldiers made them clean out bombed out buildings so the buildings could be built up and reused. They usually had to scrub bricks so they could be used to rebuild. Most of the nice houses were taken over by Czechs and Jewish people. They would nail a paper to the door and claim the homes for themselves. The owners had no rights to even enter the home again. I don't know where all of these Jews came from, they seemed to crawl out of the woodwork after the Germans ran. Not that I blamed them for hiding. I sure as heck wished we would have found a place to hide so we could have avoided those interminable months in the prison camp.

While the older prisoners were out laboring in town, the younger children were allowed to play around a bit in the camp during the day. We played some soccer and got to know the routine of our captors pretty well. Emboldened over time, we would tease the guards for entertainment. Once, while the guards were distracted by some of the children in the courtyard, my brother held up a piece of barbed wire fence for me. I slipped under the fence to pick us a couple potatoes from a small garden I had spotted and slipped back before any guards noticed. It was a pretty stupid plan, but at the time it was worth it.

It was during this time that my Aunt Mitzi, one of Ma's sisters, had pity upon us and dared to help us. She would walk back and forth along the street next to one side of the camp fence. She wore a long coat and hid a partial loaf of bread underneath. After she knew we had spotted her, she tossed the bread over the fence and kept on walking so she wouldn't draw attention to herself. My little brother and I would rush to grab the bread before anyone else could get it. It was a marvelous treat that kept us going. We would rip the bread into scraps and tuck it into our clothing so we could share it with Ma and our older brother after they returned from their labors. She did this about once a week, so I would keep my eyes peeled for her and her gracious gift.

This one small act of compassion helped to sustain me and kept the fire of hope burning within me. Even at that young age, I had witnessed enough first hand to have realized the disparity among the moral compass poised in each person's heart. I determined it was a conscious decision to determine how each would spend the precious time they have been granted on this earth. By the age of twelve I knew how tenuous life was. Some choose to run their life fueled on hate or greed or fear; I ran on hope.

A gruesome incident, forever burned into my memory, occurred on one of those days playing around in the camp courtyard. One of my new camp pals chased the ball behind the guard tower where it had rolled. His curiosity got the best of him when he stumbled upon a treasure and he called to me to look at what he had found. When I looked his direction, I saw he was holding a hand grenade up in the air with the pin pulled. I yelled for him to throw it. He listened and attempted to toss it away, but not fast enough. His entire arm from the elbow down was blown off by the blast. I ran over and knelt down next to him as he was crying for his mama. Blood was gushing from the stump that was now what was left of his arm. The guards rushed over and pushed me aside as they picked up my little buddy. I saw them carry him away, leaving a trail of blood in their wake. I never saw him again, but I am sure he died. I don't know if he even had a chance to see his ma before he died. Again, that hopeless feeling overcame me like a cloud blocking out the sun. We were just kids… what did we do to deserve this?

After that horrible hand grenade accident, the guards rounded up the young children to keep a closer eye on us. They decided to teach us Russian and Czech to keep us busy. So, for three to four hours a day they taught us how to write and speak their language. That went on for quite a while, I don't know how many months for sure because one day blurred into the next. It was at least a way to pass the time and occupy my mind. During these times of tutoring, at least they treated us with some dignity. I refused to dwell on the negative aspects of my circumstances as I concentrated on my studies and avoided the slippery slope of surrendering to despair. I always held onto the hope that things would get better.

16

Another Trip on the Rails

Finally the day came. The guards called us out and announced what we had been waiting to hear since the day we first arrived. They told us all who rejected communism could go to Bavaria. Needless to say, we were quite happy to hear this. Once again, we each publicly reaffirmed that we would not submit to communism. With that proclamation, our fate was sealed. Finally we would get out of there, but we would lose our homeland as part of the bargain. We knew we were being sent to the American zone by rail. While we didn't know exactly where the train was going, we figured anywhere was better than the damn camp.

We waited until they said our barrack could go. They then marched us out of the camp. It was a wonderful feeling walking through those gates after those long months of confinement. We must have looked like a raggedy bunch of rejects with filthy clothes hanging loose on our withered frames. Despite our gaunt appearance, the surge of expectation added a glimmer to our eyes and a slight bounce to our steps…each one taking us one step closer to freedom.

From the camp, we were marched directly to the train station. They opened the cattle cars and jammed it full of people, closed the door, then marched us to the next one. We tried to stay together; it was difficult with all of the people bunched together. Our family somehow managed to get into the same boxcar. After the car was packed to capacity, the clang of the metal door seemed to seal our destiny. We were lighthearted and eager to move on to an unknown, but better place. I don't know how long we waited as the whole freight train got loaded and started moving. The rocking of the train along the track seemed like a soothing lullaby to the load of passengers daring to hope again after all of those months.

We didn't get too far, though, before we bumped to a stop. For some reason they needed the locomotive for something else and they left us, packed like animals in boxcars, on the side rail. We were in Prague. Everything was disconnected and the locomotive chugged away from us. We sat there waiting to move again, wondering what plans they had for us. People were crying and shouting at first, but then decided to just sit there and conserve their energy. We had no food or water, nothing. We were again left with no choice in our life, except to hope that someone would eventually come for us. It was two or three days of anguish locked in that boxcar with a common feeling of desperation and anguish. No one wanted to voice their fears of dying now, after surviving those long hellish months in that camp. The stench of urine and body odor permeated the boxcar. I kept myself positioned by the outer wall and pushed my face between the small slats to breathe some fresher air. As the hours dragged on, I wondered if this was literally the end of the line.

Finally, on the third day or so, we felt the bump of the locomotive train hooking up to us. We were once again on our way to somewhere; at this point we were just happy to be moving.

We started to pull out of Prague toward the Bavaria border. I don't know how long it took, I don't think too long. The train went through the Schwartzwald and on to the German/Czech border into Bavaria. Right away when we stopped moving, the boxcar doors were slid open and we had a wonderful welcoming party. The American Red Cross was there with hot soup, potatoes, bread, and cheese, but not much meat. We were in paradise. We each got our own big cup of soup and we could even go back for seconds. After we ate our fill, they took our names, who we were and where we were from. Then, they put us on a regular passenger train. They had sent people in two different directions by pointing one there and one there. I don't know how they figured it, but they had to spread people out because of overcrowding in Bavaria from the influx of war refugees.

17

A Whisper of Freedom

We eventually ended up in Memmingen, which was in Bavaria. And boy did we luck out....we got off the train and they marched us up to an old concentration camp, but this time with the gates open. We again had a barracks but they did provide us with heat and blankets. We had a stove and cots to sleep on so it was a much better place than we had before. There were a couple of camps and various kinds of people there, so the Red Cross had set up a station in town. We had to walk to get a loaf of bread and a one-gallon can of soup. We went on a daily basis. They told us we had to stay there until they found us housing. What they did was go to all the houses in town and asked people with an extra room to give it up to us.

It took about two months and finally the good news came that they found a spot for us. It was in Kaiser Promenade. Frau Houshover was the house lady and she was in charge. She told us that we had to pay rent and had to be quiet. If we made any problems or caused any damage, she had the right to kick us out and we'd have to go back to the camp. So we did the best we could by letting our steam off somewhere else so we would not disrupt her.

The four of us lived in one upstairs' room in this house in Bavaria and felt fortunate to have it. This photo is dated 1946.

When we would go into town, we saw the bakery full of bread and a meat market full of meat. We thought we had it made, but we didn't have any money. Also, our dialect gave us away, so even if we got a little money to buy meat, they always told us they didn't have any. Or they'd just give us some tough meat or bones that were smelly already. But at least we had something. We were allowed to cook in our apartment over a stove so we could make soup or coffee. My mother got a job at a vegetable nursery; they used to grow flowers but switched to vegetables to feed all the people. She helped with planting and harvesting. Whatever produce wasn't up to par, they would sell to her at a cheaper price. So at least we had some spinach and kohlrabi. We didn't ever throw anything away, not even the leaves. We had a lot of kerdoffle soup.

As we started to get familiar with the area we began to find where we could get things on the side. We discovered a flour mill along a creek in Buksach where we walked to get a little bit of rye flour. It cost about two cents to get a half pound of the flour. It didn't look that good, like it was floor sweepings, but at least we could use it to thicken up the cooked vegetables. One thing we noticed was that the Bavarians had wonderful pets that were healthy. So, here and there we got a cat. One day I had the privilege of running into a nice dog, he was friendly and so was I. I took him into the wood shed, butchered him the best I could, and took the meat home to Ma.

Then my brother got sick, I think he had something resulting from malnutrition. He was very sick and had to go to the hospital. Since she felt he did not get fed well enough in the hospital, one day Ma took a dog leg along for my brother to eat. The aroma of the cooked meat drew the attention of the nurses who asked Ma what smelled so good. She replied that she had gotten a leg of lamb from a farmer and cooked it. The nurses ate up what my brother couldn't eat. Surprisingly, they thought it was one of the best meats they had ever eaten.

Shortly thereafter, it was my turn to get sick. When I couldn't walk upright anymore, my ma became angry with me because she thought I was being lazy. She felt I just didn't want to go out and get soup that day. After delivering a good scolding, she did finally take me to the doctor and he sent me to the hospital right away. A surgeon cut out my appendix and later reported that it was to the point of bursting. Instead of sutures, they just taped me up. I still have a nasty scar as a remembrance of this experience. I spent at least three weeks in the hospital because I got an infection. Overall, this wasn't such a bad experience. I was lucky to have survived this medical crisis and, for once, I was able to eat food which I hadn't had to find myself.

After I got out of the hospital, I started school in Memmingen. I began in the seventh grade after having missed a year and a half of school, so I had a lot of studying and make up work to do. Herr Lehrere Daniel was the teacher and he had good control of the class. He was very strict, but he made me learn quickly and catch up to the correct grade level for my age. I was tested and allowed to enter his class, but under the condition that I would be dropped to a lower grade if I couldn't cut it. He took me under his wing and pushed me to study extra hard to grasp the required skills in arithmetic, geography and social behavior. I really did not think I needed this much attention, but without realizing it I regained ground and got very good grades.

Before going to school we still ate a piece of toasted rye bread rubbed with garlic and a dash of salt. Some of the local boys, also farm boys, came to school with big meat and lard sandwiches. At lunch time, those boys ate while looking at us smiling just to make us suffer.

We had one boy in the class no one liked. His name was Otto. He was like a nerd because he was very smart. He had curly, brownish red hair and real thick glasses. He always carried money and appeared to be well off. After analyzing the situation, I thought this might be my lucky day. At that point I decided to buddy up to him. I started to talk to him in a nice way and asked where he lived. He was so happy to have someone talking to him that he invited me to his home. Wow, my eyes nearly popped out of my head gazing at what I saw there. His pantry was loaded with lard, butter, all kinds of meat and even white bread. He just gave me a knife and told me to go ahead and eat. I didn't wait to be told twice; I grabbed the knife and got busy making my feast. This day I ate the single biggest lard and meat sandwich I ever had in my life. I could hardly open my mouth big enough to bite into it. After I gorged myself, he showed me his playroom. It was located below the tile roof and was filled with games and toys I had never seen before. I was shocked as Otto explained his variety of entertainment. I couldn't believe one kid could have so much. After that, I went to play with Otto, who I called Ottie, two to three times a week. He helped me with studies and I became close to him the more I got to know him.

Ottie's father was a shoemaker and had a tiny shop in the downstairs of their home. I never saw many customers coming into this shop. There were a few getting new soles and heels put on old shoes, but no one was having new shoes made. There just wasn't the money available. It seemed funny to me that those few jobs would provide my new friend with so much food, toys and money. Finally, my curiosity got the better of me and I asked him where his father made all the money. At first he told me just to enjoy his friendship. Then, one day, he opened up to me. He confided that his father did special favors for Jews and that's where most of the money came from. He made me swear never to reveal to anyone what it was, but I knew and it has haunted me.

Shortly after that revelation, I was relocated to work on a farm and never saw Ottie again. Before I left, Ottie brought me a handmade pair of ski boots made special for me by his father. This effort was expended because I was the best friend his son ever had. He made them a couple of sizes bigger, so I could wear them a long time as I grew into them.

When I told Herr Daniel I had to go to the farm he actually cried. He told me he was so mean to me because otherwise I might have slacked off. He had recognized my quick mind and knew I had great potential. He asked me to reconsider leaving so I could continue with my studies. I explained that I had to go because of the food situation and that this would be the best for my family. He left me with one final lesson. As he firmly shook my hand in farewell, he looked me straight in the eyes and said, "Always look forward, never back." I thanked him and walked out of the classroom without a backward glance. I left with a lump in my throat because of the depth of his words. This was a totally new concept for me to digest. I was struck with the sincerity of his teary-eyed message and was amazed at the realization that he had been tough on me because he believed in me.

18

Life as a Cowboy

I began my work out on a farm after recuperating from surgery for five months, making friends with Ottie and mastering the objectives of seventh grade. My ma told me they needed a cowboy but warned me that I had to be a real good catholic because the family was very Christian. She took me out on the train, about fifteen miles outside of town to meet this family. I wore my best pair of shorts at the time, a green shirt, and I was taken out to see the farmer. I was given a thorough inspection when I arrived. It was similar to a job interview for a position I honestly didn't want any part of. The farmer, Herr Johann Bauer, told me they needed someone to watch the cows and briefly explained the duties. This farmer was one of the richer farmers in Illerbeuren, with forty cows and five horses. I was approved for the job and my ma was told I could start right away. Just like that, I transferred my school out of

HANS

Memmigen and left my family behind. I was not quite 12 years old when I got kicked out of the nest and put right to work. I started in February. In a way I wished I could have stayed home, but I knew food was so short. With me out of the house, they were able to keep my food stamps for themselves. So, for the sake of my family, I bravely stayed at the farm and started working.

I cried myself to sleep for the first week, but then got into the routine and made the best of it. I had my own room over the horses and cows in the barn. My bed was a straw sack that got changed once a year when the rye was harvested. They harvested the rye with a sickle and thrashed it by hand to keep the stalks nice and long. We would stuff these stalks into the sack and stitch the bag back up. At first, I just about rolled off of the mound. But, after a couple of nights I hollowed a dip in the middle to form my cocoon. The combination of a feather bed cover and the heat from the manure and animals below kept me warm all winter.

The farmer was a widower with three daughters and two sons in his family. I was the only hired hand. It was a crew of hunchbacks and all of them had a gullet flapping beneath their chin. I am not exaggerating to say I was the best looking of the bunch. The boys were named Franz and Sebastian. The girls were Mina, Cecil, & Fanni. The girls were a bunch of old maids. Fanni was the oldest and she directed all of the housework. The girls' chores included feeding the chickens, gathering eggs, cooking, baking, and working out in the fields.

LIFE AS A COWBOY

This is a photo taken on my Confirmation Day in 1947. I am standing between Ma and my sponsor, Sebastian (one of the hunch backs).

I had a hand in helping the women bake bread every three weeks. The starter sourdough was activated the night before to create enough for twenty-one dough balls. In the morning, twenty of these balls were allowed to rise and one was put back into the cupboard to use as starter for next time. Before I took the cows to pasture, I crawled inside the cool oven to stack the two-foot logs in a tic-tac-toe pattern. The fire was started with a bit of dried twigs in the middle. This would create an even fire that burned down to embers. At this point, the women would scrape out the coals and sweep the oven clean with a broom. With a flat floured wooden board, they would place the risen dough balls into the heated bake oven. Besides the sourdough loaves, they also baked some flat bread sprinkled with salt and caraway seed as a special treat. This sort of tasted like a pretzel with a nutty flavor. The finished loaves of bread were stored in the pantry and reheated as needed. The fresh bread was the best, because the crust thickened over time and got pretty hard by the end of three weeks.

Once a week I got a bath, I was seventh in line for the bath, which was a wooden barrel. Herr Bauer got the first bath, then the daughters, then the sons, and then me. Everyone got an extra pitcher of hot water added to the bath water. Sometimes I felt that I came out dirtier than when I went in, but at least I got a bath. In the summer, I would mostly go into the river to swim, so I really didn't need a bath anyway.

I wore hand me downs from Franz who was the slimmer of the sons. This was the first pair of long pants I ever wore. I held them up with suspenders. I always was barefoot except for the time I was in the barn milking. The home-made milking shoes looked a bit like modern day crocs. The soles were fashioned out of wood and covered with a leather tip to cover the toes. They were one size fits all. If one of the cows were sick, we had to disinfect the shoes with an ammonia dip to prevent the illness from spreading to the entire herd. If a farm was discovered to have hoof and mouth disease, the entire farm was quarantined until cleared by a vet. During this time, neither the milk nor the animals could be sold. To keep my bare feet warm in the winter, I stood in the warm piles of manure.

My normal day started with getting kicked out of bed at 4:30 a.m. One of the daughters would yell, "Hans, mach schnell." In response, I jumped out of bed, put on my clothes and got to work. I started by cleaning and feeding the horses. Then it was time to milk the cows. They gave me a couple older ones at first to learn, then, in no time I worked my way up to milk seven cows. After that, I could go to breakfast where I sat at my assigned chair. We ate mŭs, which consisted of coarsely ground wheat that was cooked in 1/2 milk and 1/2 water in a huge frying pan. This big copper pan was set in the middle of the table and everyone used their spoon to dig into the two-inch deep mŭs, with a consistency resembling oatmeal. When that was gone, a bowl of coffee was brought out with cut bread in it. Again, everyone dug into the same common bowl. It was actually quite good. We had to lick the spoon clean when finished and place it in the cubby hole below the table top. The spoon was never washed, just licked. When the food was gone, we headed back out to work. I learned not be shy about eating my share because once it was gone, it was gone. It took longer to say the prayer than it did to eat.

Then I would have to take the milk to the creamery which was famous for limburger and Swiss cheese. I had to carefully push a two-wheel cart that held one big kettle of fresh milk. The creamery was about a half mile away and it would take me twenty minutes to get there. After the cheese man weighed the milk and dumped it into a big vat, I rinsed the bucket and ran back to the farm. There I switched kettles and went back to the creamery for whey. The cheese man was quite old, he knew I was skinny and he told me to drink a 1/2 cup of the whey, cheese water, every day and I would get healthy. It didn't taste good at all, but after a while I got used to it and even looked forward to it.

I took the kettle full of whey back to the farm and used this to feed the pigs and cows. The whey would be dumped into the feeding troughs running lengthwise through the barn. The pigs would also be fed a half bucket of ground barley. We had to ration this out so they would grow slowly so the butchered meat would be better when the time came. The pigs would be butchered when they were eighteen months old and weighing about 540 lbs. It depended upon the time of year, how the cows' food was supplemented. In the winter, they were fed hay and sliced beets. In the summer, they were taken to pasture after drinking the whey and water.

So, during the summer months, I would head out to the fields with the cows. I would put the bells on the cows and lead them out to pasture. Each cow had a different bell. The lead cow showed everyone the way after I opened the gate. She had the biggest bell and all of the other cows fell into line behind her. The rest of my day was spent out in the pasture overseeing the cows. I would make sure they ate in designated areas, in a specific pattern to allow the grass to keep growing all summer long. I also had to make sure they wouldn't over eat. If a cow's belly would start to bloat, I had to run the whole herd home early to save the cow. In this case, we had to use a special tool to punch a hole in the cow's belly to allow the gas to escape. After the pressure was relieved, the hole would be covered with lard and the cow would be saved from death.

Over time I made friends with a young cow so I could drink right out of her tits. We were buddies, I would share my apple with the cow and she would share her milk with me. I would lay under her and spray the milk into my mouth. The farmer always wondered why that one cow didn't have more milk. I was given a burlap lunch sack to take along with me to pasture. It consisted of a piece of rye bread, an apple and a jug of cider. I could refill this jug out of a naturally flowing spring in the pasture, so I had plenty to drink all day long.

After about six hours, I would open the log gate and yell, "Ho, ho, ho." This would signal the cows to head back home to the barn. The cows had to be milked at a precise time in both the morning and the evening. After the return to the barn, I would add water to the trough so they could drink up to milking time. Right after the evening milking, I would push the wagon transporting the can of milk to the creamery again. I would not have to return for the whey at the end of the day; we only got that once a day. I would run the cart back to the farm, wash the container and get it ready for the next morning.

At dark, it was time for supper. I washed up a little and headed back to my chair and spoon. For dinner, there was usually a big bowl of vegetable soup in the middle of the table with sliced rye bread. On rare occasions, there was a bowl of stew with potatoes. On the farm, we all ate off the same platter or serving bowl except for on Sunday. On Sunday, we each got our own plate and the food was heartier with more meat and bigger portions. Supper concluded with rosary prayers that lasted about fifteen minutes. If there were any extra chores to finish, like watching a cow ready to calve, I wasn't finished for the day until after they were completed. If no additional chores were assigned, I was officially done until morning. I usually crawled back into bed by 8:00 p.m. or so, depending upon the time of year. I had no light in my room so I slept based upon the cycle of the sun. I was exhausted and slept well.

My day also included a variety of other chores. I repaired fences, rakes and a multitude of farm tools. I cleaned out the chicken coop and pig pen once a week. The cow manure was pushed into a pit and water was flushed into it to liquefy it. I had to use a big plunger to mix it up good so it would easily flow into a big tank beneath the manure pile outside. This liquid manure was then spread onto the fields with a wooden mistbreiter, like a modern day honey wagon pulled by a horse. The grain crops included barley, oats, wheat and rye. During harvest time, Franz or Sebastin would cut swatches of it down with a horse drawn mowing machine. The girls and I followed behind to bundle up the stalks with the grain on it. We stood them up like little puppets throughout the field. After a day of drying, we collected these stacks onto a flat wagon and hauled them to the barn. During poor weather, usually in the late fall, we would thrash the grain. The bagged grain, in 200-pound bags, was hauled up to the third floor of the barn to be used for feed and to make flour. Any extra, was taken to market and sold. The remaining straw was tossed loose up to the hay loft in the barn. I would be positioned up high to pack the straw tightly up to the roof. No space was wasted. One side was used for straw and the other for hay.

Once a week I churned butter in the evening before heading to bed. The cream was dumped into the butter churn. I would turn the geared crank that moved the wooden paddles inside. This motion churned the cream into butter after about ninety minutes of constant cranking. The butter was stored on the floor where the coolness would keep it from spoiling. There was never any ice, except during the winter. I would watch the women mend clothes or knit socks as I did this chore because I didn't have any light in my room. The women would sing old Bavarian folk songs as they worked, so at least this task was entertaining.

My most hated job was associated with the calving process. In the event the cow didn't eliminate the afterbirth, I was sent in to retrieve it. I was elected for this job because of my long, skinny arms. In preparation, I had to cut my fingernails short, take off my shirt and grease up my arm with a stinky antiseptic solution. Someone would stabilize the cow and hold the tail out of the way. I then had to slip my entire arm, up to my armpit, inside the cow and reach my fingers around to scrape off the remaining afterbirth. I would gag and vomit from the stench as I stood behind the cow doing this horrible task. Afterward, I had to reach back in and apply a handful of antiseptic so the cow didn't get an infection.

I was granted home leave about once a month for a period of two days. I peddled one of the girls' bikes the fifteen miles home. This took me about two hours and I traveled with patches and an air pump in case I got a flat tire. As I would enter town; all the people would turn away because they could smell the stink of the cow shit on me. Even though I changed into my city clothes, they could detect that I was a farmer from 10-15 yards away. In the summer it smelled a little bit more because all of the manure was kept in pits below where the cows were housed. This gave off a real rosy aroma. After a while I couldn't even smell it, but other people sure could. During this period of one night and two days away, Ma first made me take a good bath and washed my clothes to kill the smell a bit. I didn't do too much. I would maybe go to a movie, but I didn't really have any money unless Ma gave me some. There was one movie theater in town that cost about 80 Fennig, or 20 cents, to attend. I would only go if there was a cowboy or pirate movie showing. I didn't care to see any love stories.

After the first year of work out there, I had the chance to make my younger brother as happy as I was by finding him a job as a cowboy too. He ended up working for a farmer in the same village, located closer to the creamery. At least then I had someone to visit with while delivering the milk. My older brother had been working as a tinsmith and wasn't very healthy. For my labors, my mother got paid once a year. After the first year of service she got paid the equivalency of twelve and half-dollars and a dozen eggs. The farmer informed her, "Hans is too weak to do a man's job." That bastard used this as an excuse to not pay her much for my year round, sunrise to sunset labors. I never saw any of the money from my labors anyway, so I guess it really didn't matter. Ma took the money to buy medicine and things for my older brother.

HANS

This photo of the two "cowboys" was taken behind Herr Bauer's farm in 1947. I was 13 years old and my younger brother was 10. We were happy to spend some time together.

The second year on the farm there were more complicated chores added to the basics I already did. This included plowing the fields with the horses or cutting the hay. We would plant feed beets by hand, one at a time. During the winter we would make the farm tools, all by hand, to prepare for the next season. We built hay sticks, rakes and handles for the hoes. The local blacksmith, called the schmied, not only made the horseshoes but also fashioned axes, beet forks and the ends of the hoes out of steel to the farmers liking. All of the handles were made by us out of hardwood. There were always things to repair and I kept very busy throughout the winter months. Of course, there were always the cows to milk twice a day and the animals to feed. I also would have to go into the woods to cut pine logs for fencing and split them with wedges. The same process was used to collect fire wood. In the spring, I cut down brush near the river to make brooms. They didn't buy these things; they were all made "in house." So, in a way, it was quite an experience, but I sure wouldn't have gotten rich there.

I stayed there for another year and then I got lucky. A butcher shop needed someone that could take care of cows and I was promised a job. I informed the farmer, Herr Johann Bauer that I would be done on the second day of February. It was only on this day, called lichtmess (which is known as Groundhog Day in America), that we were allowed to switch jobs for a better position. He got mad and yelled and carried on. He said that they fed me all winter while there wasn't much work to do and then I was going to leave. This wasn't true, because I worked steady all winter long while he played cards in the restaurant bar. I mutely accepted his anger and burst of yelling, then happily departed when February 2nd arrived. Herr Bauer gave me nothing for send off, but his children did. They gave me ten marcs each when I left and wished me well on my new position. I used this money to purchase the necessary tools for my new trade which included knives, boots and an apron. (A few years ago I visited this farm and Herr Bauer's burial plot in Bavaria. I wanted to pay my respects, but my wife wouldn't let me take a piss on his grave.)

19

Learning a Trade

When I started my butchering career, I had to sign a three-year contract. This contract was a commitment to learn the sausage making and butchering trade. For this apprenticeship, I made what amounted to 75-cents a week for all the work that was required. The contract also included a stipulation that I would get a formal education in the trade school for three years. This class met once a week for five hours. During class I was taught many important aspects of the trade. I learned what diseases looked like and how to detect them in the carcasses. I learned trouble shooting measures to ensure the highest quality finished product. For instance, I was taught to use very sharp knives or blades in the meat chopper to process the meat so it wouldn't get mushy. I was introduced to the process of using ice to cool the meat which was totally new to me. I really enjoyed these classes and paid close attention to learn the technical aspects.

HANS

I ended up working about 80 hours a week. I would start the day by getting the fire going under the kettle, then head out to milk and feed the cows. After the milking, I would take the trip to the creamery to deliver the milk. In the summer I had to go twice a day because the milk would sour, but in the winter I could go once a day. It was pretty tough to be the beginner or lehrling for three years while aspiring to be a journeyman. It was my job to do all of the work from cleaning the casings to delivering the meat to the slaughter house and various restaurants. It was a small butcher shop so we did a couple pigs a week and maybe a small calf every other week. We would sometimes split work with the other butcher shops when a steer or bull was butchered. All of the meat had to be hauled back and forth from the slaughterhouse on a hand wagon about three miles away. This was necessary because we didn't have a good cooling system right at the shop. I was the designated errand boy.

Part of my contract stated the butcher would provide room and board for me. After staying about six weeks in a small room on the third floor above the butcher shop, I talked them into letting me stay with my family instead. This was a much better arrangement for me. Since I could sleep at home, they would give me a sandwich every night but nothing for breakfast. I would just grab a cup of coffee at home before I headed to work about half a mile away. For lunch, I would usually have some old sausage that was a little gray that they didn't want to sell. That was also my sandwich at night with a couple pieces of rye bread.

Over time I made friends with the journeyman. His name was Eric. When we tied the sausages, the master butcher would stand behind us. He was the owner of the house and his name was Herr Lutzenberger. He was seventy-five years old, very slow and fat. He would watch us and count, so we didn't sneak any sausages for ourselves. If one would bust, he would get mad and I would get slapped across the face. This helped me to stay focused and try not to mess up. I learned to multi-task between keeping the kettle of water at the correct temperature of 160-180 degrees, keeping the proper temperature in the smoke house, cutting meat, stuffing sausage, and measuring spices. After supervising an hour or two, Herr Lutzenberger would either go upstairs to sleep or help his wife sell the meat and sausage in the butcher shop out front. Then, without him watching our every move Eric ran the show.

Eric was a very smart man who took me under his wing and taught me much-not all of it about butchering. We would sometimes re-tie some sausages to make them a little smaller so we could each eat a fresh one without the owner missing it. He also filled me in on the fun we could have catching our own game. The next building was a bakery which I had to visit once a week so they could bake the pans with the leberkäse, similar to bologna loaf, in it. I would return in two hours to pick it back up. This drove the business for the baker as well, because people would buy a roll to put a slab of hot leberkäse on to make a sandwich. Well, the bakery had a pigeon coop on top. Eric was quite good with the sling shot and, thanks to his idea, I got one too. We made a habit of using the pigeons for target practice. Once a week we would get two or three of the neighbor's pigeons and that would make a good pigeon noodle soup at home. We didn't want to take too many, because the neighbor might miss them. Since we were smart about it, the neighbor just complained that some of his homing pigeons were stupid and didn't find their way back home.

At that time, everything was put into the sausage. It was amazing what could be put in there- head skin, feet, bone meal off of the saw – were all utilized to create sausage. When we cooked the meat that wasn't used for sausage, this cooking water would be sold. This was called "Kessel Suppe" or kettle soup. The owner's wife would sell it to people and she had two separate pots to choose between. The one pot was for Flüchtlinge, which was what they called the deported people like us who relocated to the area. The town folk hated the Flüchtlinge because they felt they disrupted their lifestyle. So, the Flüchtlinge would get the watered down version of the Kessel Suppe. The good customers-which was meant to be the locals- would get the good stuff. At the time, I learned that the people in town got the preferred grade of meat, bones, vegetables and the best soup available, all for the same price as the

Flūchtlinge. Basically, the Flūchtlinge didn't have much choice, they were happy with what they got and made the best of it.

We were still on stamps at that time. I would take any extra bones I could get. One day I was walking up the alley with the hand wagon with not much meat on it, and I saw a big cat run across my path. Not one to pass up an opportunity, I pushed the handle against the fence so the wagon wouldn't roll down the alley. I grabbed my sling-shot and hit the cat right before he could stick his head through the fence and escape. Then, I grabbed it, killed it and put it under the tarp. I skinned it out at the shop right away and snuck up to the nearby tannery to process the hide. When I went in there, the woman yelled for her sister and told her what a beautiful fur it was, just like her kitty. I was scared, and said, "No, no, no, it is from my aunt across town." They gave me two marks, which was almost a week's wages, just for the fur of their own cat. As a bonus, I got to eat the meat too. I was scared to go down that path anymore, because it went right past the tannery. I wanted to avoid it so they wouldn't see me again. I feared that I might be either beat up or put in jail. From then on, I had to go an extra half-mile on every trip, but, in a way, it was worth it.

Another day, I saw a dog come running along as I walked home from work. I gave him a piece of my sand-wich so he followed me right home to the wood shed. I had no problem dispatching the critter. From my experience, everything was fair game and the name of the game was survival. So, every once in a while we had extra meat to eat and I was able to get even with the Bavarian hosts by taking care of their pets.

During our stay in Memmingen, we began to write to my mother's sister, my aunt, in America. In these letters, we explained that we sure would like to come to America. According to the laws, as "displaced persons" the government would pay our passage if we could get sponsors in America. We discovered from the American Embassy located in Munich that we had a real chance to relocate. So, we kept working on the papers both through the official channels in Munich and in America. The time stretched out as we waited.

We hit the jackpot after my third year as a butcher's apprentice. In July, 1951, we received notices in the same week that we were approved to immigrate to either America or Australia. At this point, we had a choice in deciding our future. Everyone in the family agreed they wanted to go to America. We thought we had a rich aunt there who would help us get started in our new homeland. It was a surreal time. While I could hardly believe my dream was coming true, I was also afraid something would screw things up.

We were notified that we needed to report to an U.S. Army base in Munich in September of 1951. I was 17 years old at that time. When I told this to the new owner of the shop, who I was currently working under, he was quite upset because he liked my work. After he settled down, he begrudgingly agreed to help me take my journeyman's test before I immigrated. This was four months earlier than originally scheduled. The three-day test included a lot of work to prove I had mastered all of the necessary skills to be a journeyman butcher. I had to make four different varieties of sausage, butcher a pig, skin out a calf and complete a written test. I did manage to successfully complete each of these requirements and got my journeyman's papers. The papers were made official by the signatures of the two master butchers, one journeyman, and the professor of the trade school who all awarded me a passing grade. This paperwork was important to me, because if America wouldn't have worked out or if I didn't pass the physical, at least I could have gotten another job as a journey butcher. Without the papers, I would have had to start all over.

Prior to leaving Bavaria, I successfully acquired my butcher journeyman certification. In addition, my older brother had received his journeyman as a tinsmith and my younger brother had a year in as an apprentice with a baker making dough, pretzels and assorted pastries. Throughout this time period, my ma was working at the brewery and received wooden tokens for discounted beer. Despite the less than hospitable stint in Bavaria, we were appreciative of the opportunities offered. Bavaria allowed us to each learn a trade to enhance our chances for a brighter future.

20

The Voyage "Home"

The official process required that we receive a physical prior to the final authorization for immigration. We traveled to Munich by train to receive this physical. I was really worried that my sickly older brother would not pass. At this point, we also had to take an oath that we were not communist and did not belong to a political action group. The agreement included a clause stating we would serve in the U.S. armed forces for a period of at least two years to fulfill our end of the bargain. In addition, we would be granted a period of five years to become fluent in the English language in order to be awarded U.S. citizenship. We returned home to Bavaria to await notification of approval after a background check was completed on each of us. It took two months of sweating it out until we received the official approval and instructions on how to proceed.

It was around the 24th of November when we left

for Munich by train to return to the U.S. Army base for processing. We were each allowed 40 kilos, or about 80 pounds, of baggage per person. We had to pay our own way to board the train for Munich to get to the base. Once again, my family and I boarded a train with great expectations. We had kept this single hope alive through all of the years of the aggravation. We arrived at the U.S. Army base and we were assigned a barrack where we would stay while all the tests were done. The tests included chest x-rays, blood work, and a physical exam to check our health status. By completing this portion in Munich, we didn't have to stay at Ellis Island in New York upon our arrival to America. After about a weeks' time, we were given the final stamp of approval. We were then told that we would be heading for Bremen where a ship was waiting for us.

This is my passport photo which was taken in 1951 in preparation for my journey to America. I was 17 years old.

The Army bus took us to the train station in Munich where we joined our traveling companions to the new land. As the train approached the harbor, we spotted the biggest ship I'd ever seen. It was a troop transporter named the U.S.S. General Sturgis. We disembarked the train and walked right to the ship. It was the third of December, 1951, when I boarded the ship headed to America. It was already loaded and we were the last batch of passengers to get on board. We hand carried enough clothing for fourteen days, the estimated travel time, and the rest of our baggage was stowed in the ship's baggage area.

After we boarded the ship, we were told that we would be assigned a work detail for the voyage. This was necessary because they were short of help, crewmembers, with all of the immigrants on board. I volunteered to be a cook, since I was a butcher, and that was quite welcomed by the crew. My brother was assigned to be a guard for the baggage area and was given a club to carry. My younger brother got off cheap and didn't have to work at all. The reason was he was small and only about 15 years of age at that time. Ma did some cleaning in the passenger cabin as her work duty.

So, on the third day of December, 1951, we departed Bremer hafen for America. We were all so happy to get underway. When we got out to sea, though, it was really rough. There were many storms since it was December. Most of the passengers, even some of the crew, got sick during the voyage. With every new storm, another wave of vomiting erupted from the seasick passengers. The sour stench of vomit permeated the passageways.

My job was to be a cook's assistant. The worst part of this job was the smell of powdered eggs, which emitted a rotten, pungent odor. We had to use the powdered eggs for breakfast after we ran out of the real ones about eight days out to sea. The other regular items served for breakfast included ham, potatoes and toast. This was the normal meal for passengers and crew. I was peeling potatoes, wow, what a bunch of potatoes. It took me about four hours a day to peel enough potatoes for everyone. After the potatoes were done, the cooks would bring in whole hams or beef roasts. It was my job to trim them out. These large portions of meat would be roasted for three to four hours in the big ovens located in the kitchen. The completed food was shipped upstairs via the dumbwaiter where it was served. I had never laid eyes on so much food in my life.

The passengers and crewmembers had one menu and the cooks and officers had another one-which was much better. The cooks in the kitchen had their own stash of food. This included fresh eggs for the entire voyage, bacon, hash browns, toast, orange juice, and premium coffee for breakfast. For lunch and dinner we got the meat tenderloins reserved for us and a lot of fresh vegetables. I was taught how to butterfly the tenderloins and wrap them in bacon, holding it in place with toothpicks. The cooks would then broil them and serve them smothered in onions. This was my first experience eating an American steak, it was unbelievably delicious. The cooks and the officers all ate in their own mess hall located on the floor below the regular dining room. I was in heaven since before this I couldn't even get close to any food like this. I was used to tough old beef, so the first time I tried steaks like these it was amazing.

Everyday I would report to the kitchen by 5:00 a.m. and I'd be done at night after I finished washing dishes. It would be late at night when I got done. I would crawl up into my bunk and fall into an exhausted, but satisfied, sleep. My bed was located on the top of rows of bunks stacked four high. I remember that the cabins weren't small, they were bigger rooms than I had expected to find on a ship. We all had our own assigned bunk to sleep in, but sometimes we could hardly stay in bed due to the rocking of the ship. During the worst storms they would make us stay below, because they were afraid that we would get washed overboard. I took one peek out of the port hole and saw waves washing right over the top of the ship. The ship looked so big when we boarded it in Breman that I never thought that a wave would go over it, but they sure did. The squeaking of the ship made me fear it would sink before I ever stepped foot in America. I prayed that I would survive this final leg of my journey to freedom.

The ship suffered mechanical damage which further hindered our voyage. One of the screws to the propellers broke. Without this propeller, we lost the capacity to steer into the waves to diminish the rocking action. The crewmen assured us they would correct it, but it took a total of two days to get the necessary repairs completed to regain optimal steering operations. The crewmembers confided in me that this was one of the worst Atlantic crossings the ship ever undertook.

All of a sudden, early one morning, everyone began shouting. We had arrived in New York Harbor and the Statue of Liberty was out there holding the torch in welcome. Everyone was shouting and scrambling for a spot by the rail to see the vision with their own eyes. We all cried when we passed under the Statute of Liberty, it was all lit up, seemingly glowing just for us. It was a moment of extreme happiness that nearly eclipsed all of the heartache endured up to that point of my life. We had left on December 3rd and arrived in New York harbor on December 17th, 1951.

So much was running through my mind as I stood at the rail smelling the sweet air of freedom. Wow, I was finally in the great big land that I had dreams about for so many years. My dreams included fantastic stories of cowboys and Indians roaming the Wild West in the ultimate land of freedom. I saw it as a marvelous adventure and I was ready to grab onto the reins and enjoy the ride. Ma was worried we would all get scalped by the Indians after we arrived, but she had already decided the risk was worth taking. It was quite a sight to see the New York skyline from my spot next to the rail. My first impression was that it was huge. I had never seen buildings like that in my life. I was stupefied by the sight.

The U.S.S. General Sturgis eased into one of the harbor slips. We watched as the gangplank was secured. We gathered our family together and crossed the gangplank when the order was granted. At that point we left the ship and stepped into a massive warehouse. The baggage was stacked into the middle of the warehouse and we had to find those that belonged to us. Standing there amongst so many people, I felt very small.

I have to admit that I was a little bit worried. We were told in a letter that our cousin would pick us up, but we didn't know if he could find us in this big warehouse. We didn't even know what he looked like and all he had was a picture of Ma. I don't know how long we waited with our bags looking around, but all of a sudden a big guy walked up to us and asked my mother if she was who he was looking for, and she said yes. Amazingly, it was my American cousin. He had traveled by car from Michigan to get us in New York. It was unbelievable to me that we actually connected.

My cousin led us to his vehicle and we loaded the bags in the trunk. I crawled into the backseat of his big American car and headed off to a new destination, my new home, with hope shining bright in my tear-welled eyes. As I peered out of the back window of the big four-door Ford, I caught sight of train tracks disappearing into the horizon. It was at that moment I realized how far I had come from my apartment window thirteen years earlier. Having my father with me would have made the moment complete. I said a silent prayer of thanksgiving as the car

HANS

rumbled on toward a place I had only envisioned in my dreams. Finally, I relaxed and allowed the soothing, welcoming warmth surround me as my new homeland enveloped me.

Epilogue

I was one of the losers. All along I never quite fit into the mold society was trying to press upon me. Shlesien, or Sudetenland, was known throughout history to have fights over the land and over everything. When Hitler finally took over, I never knew or had a clue, of what they did to the Jews. I heard stories about gas chambers after the crossing to America, but I had no first hand knowledge of what was going on. I do know it wasn't just Jews that were persecuted. It was an unwritten rule that anyone who was against Germans or their vision of a perfect race, ended up in concentration camps or dead. From their perspective, if you weren't for them-just wanting to stay on the sideline-you were against them and the status of life changed. I always felt that we suffered as much or more than a lot of them, and that opinion stems from my personal experience.

HANS

Even while leaving, it seemed as though there were a lot more survivors than ever actually went to the camps. Some things happened that I prefer not to disclose because I still have an unshakable fear that retribution will be taken against my family. But they sure made us miserable since the time Hitler took over through the period Hitler took off when the Germans lost the war. Somehow, we always found ourselves on the loser's end of the stick. I have heard many news discussions about the Jews with debates about what happened and how bad it was for them. Yet, I have never heard anybody from my position tell their story and describe the things I had to go through to survive. I had made up my mind at a tender age that we just had to survive, and survive we did.

I still think a lot of people don't appreciate America the way I do. I'm just thankful that I can be sitting here and for the opportunity I have had to make a better life. I know I won't sleep tonight, thinking about all of this, a lot more happened, you're bound to forget some things, but many things are imbedded in me. Some times I go back and think about the bad days, how bad it was and what all happened. I know that we-my family, my friends and I- lived in a constant state of fear. Like a caustic acid, fear eats away at one's very soul if left unchecked by the redemptive salve of hope. Despite the pain, it cheers me up for being here in America because I fully realize how good I have it and how good this country has been to me.

EPILOGUE

After I was living two to three years in America, we finally heard from the German Reich that my father was killed by gorillas on his way back from Greece. Out of his whole battalion, only two or three guys survived. One man from Austria signed off and told them the news. Somehow, he had a list of those in his battalion and mentioned that all the men on that list were shot in some area on the way back. By then it was too late to gather more information. Because so much time had gone by, we were unable to contact the man to find out where they were ambushed and buried. To this day, my father's disappearance remains a deep mystery to me. It is a question mark, a void in my life that has never been completely filled.

HANS

This photo is dated 1956. It was taken during my two-year career in the U.S. Army.

In fulfillment of the immigration contract, my family completed our promised obligations. My older brother was drafted into the U.S. Army in 1953. He ended up getting his U.S. citizenship in Korea before he was positioned on the front line. My younger brother finished high school and went on to college forever, until he re-

EPILOGUE

tired. Because he was a professional student, he never had to serve in the Army. I voluntarily joined the U.S. Army on May 10, 1955 and served for two years. While enlisted, they would not allow me to go overseas because there was no war and I was not an official American. I worked for and received my high school diploma while in the Army. When I received an honorable discharge on May 9, 1957, I returned to Frankenmuth, Michigan to ask for my sweetheart's hand in marriage. I became a U.S. citizen in June of 1957 and was married in November of that same year.

This is a photo taken the day I married my beautiful bride in November of 1957.

HANS

Since then, I have never asked for assistance or sympathy from anyone. I have made my own way. I refused to become a burden to America, ever. It is the cry of my heart that the foundation of America will hold strong and never succumb to the bitter forces of socialism that had thrown its dark, smothering shadow over my homeland. I pray no American child will have to stand next to the wash kettle and bear witness as the final remnant of freedom turns to ash.

I will never forget the gnawing hunger for food and a craving for a concept I could not verbalize, but for which I sought with what became an uncrushable hope for freedom and, ultimately, a chance to begin a new life in America. This was the land of opportunity, a dream I dared to hope for, yet never expected to be fully realized. I had read books about cowboys in the Wild West and imagined how wonderful it would be to live in such a free, liberated country where even a lost soul like me could make something of himself if he wanted it badly enough. Like a life line cast across the troubled seas, I grasped onto the dream and have not failed to appreciate the opportunities that have unfolded before me. I have a beautiful wife with whom I have built a life I cherish. I have four children in whom I have cultivated a drive to be self-reliant and a deep-seated gratitude for being Americans. The existence of my eight grandchildren and two great-grandchildren has assured me that a nugget of my life's legacy will flourish within them. I proudly

EPILOGUE

fly the USA flag and I thank God every day for being a citizen of America, the greatest country in the world. Not the land of my birth; but, undeniably, the land of my heart.

References:

Jablonski, E. (1977). *A Pictorial History of the World War II Years*. New York: Wings Books.

Spielvogael, J. (2006). *Western Civilization*. Canada: Thompson Corporation.

CPSIA information can be obtained
at www.ICGtesting.com
Printed in the USA
LVOW04s1106061116
511835LV00009B/575/P

NOV 16 2016